# SONIC SERENITY

## HARNESSING SOUND FOR STRESS RELIEF

## DR. MINAKSHI BANSAL

## DEDICATION


*To the quiet whispers of the heart that guide us toward inner peace.*


ᐅᐅᐅ

# Contents

# Contents

# Contents

# Prayer

*"Om Bhadram Karnebhih Shrinuyama Devah*

*Bhadram Pashyemakshabhiryajatrah*

*Sthirairangais Tushtuvamsastanubhih*

*Vyashema Devahitam Yadayuh*

*Svasti Na Indro Vriddhashravah*

*Svasti Nah Pusha Vishwavedah*

*Svasti Nastarkshyo Arishtanemih*

*Svasti No Brihaspatir Dadhatu*

*Om Shantih Shantih Shantih"*

*This mantra is a prayer for universal well-being, invoking the blessings of various deities for protection, health, and happiness. It emphasizes the importance of experiencing the auspicious through all senses and living a life aligned with divine purpose. The repetition of "Shantih" at the end signifies a deep desire for peace in the individual, the environment, and the universe at large. This mantra is often recited as a prayer for peace, prosperity, and the physical and spiritual well-being of all beings.*

ᙏᙏᙏ

# About The Author

This book represents the culmination of extensive research and meticulous analysis, incorporating a diverse range of sources, including numerous books, scholarly studies, and personal experiences. Additionally, I have scoured various websites to gather relevant information and data essential for the compilation of this work. I have taken every precaution to ensure the accuracy of the information presented and have diligently cited all sources to acknowledge their contributions.

From her earliest days, Minakshi was distinguished by an insatiable appetite for reading. Her literary universe was inhabited by characters and narratives that spanned ethical tales, motivational and inspirational stories, and the mythic parables imbued with life lessons. This voracious reading habit was not merely for personal edification but was driven by a desire to distill and disseminate the essence of these narratives to foster the development of students and peers alike. She was particularly captivated by the lives and teachings of historical figures and spiritual leaders such as Adi Shankaracharya, Swami Vivekananda, Dr. APJ Abdul Kalam, Mahamana Pandit Madan Mohan Malviya, Mahatma Gandhi, Sardar Vallabhai Patel, and Vinoba Bhave, among others. Their philosophies and life stories fueled her ambition to embody their ideals of resilience, selflessness, and relentless pursuit of knowledge.

Dr. Minakshi's academic and practical engagement with psychology has been equally noteworthy. As a research scholar, her focus has been on exploring the intricate tapestry of the human psyche, aiming to unlock the potential for psychological well-being and societal harmony. Her scholarly work is complemented by her active involvement in social work, where she employs her academic insights to make tangible differences in the lives of the underprivileged. Her endeavours in social work are characterized by an innovative approach that combines traditional wisdom with contemporary psychological practices to address the multifaceted challenges faced by these communities.

Her artistic talents, another facet of her diverse capabilities, are not merely a personal passion but also serve as a medium through which she communicates and connects with others. Her art, rich in symbolism and emotional depth, reflects her philosophical inquiries and social concerns, offering viewers a glimpse into the breadth of her intellect and the depth of her compassion.

In addition to her contributions to the arts and social sciences, Dr. Minakshi has embraced the healing arts of Pranic Healing, mastering the techniques developed by Master Choa Kok Sui. This practice, which focuses on the manipulation of Prana or life energy to heal the body and aura, has been both a personal journey of discovery and a means through which she extends her healing touch to others. Her proficiency in Pranic Healing is complemented by her advocacy and teaching of various forms of meditation aimed at rejuvenation, personal betterment, and the cultivation of harmony within individuals and communities alike.

Dr. Minakshi's life is a narrative of relentless pursuit, not just of personal achievement but of the upliftment and empowerment of society at large. Her diverse interests and talents—spanning the arts, literature, psychology, and the healing practices—converge on a singular path of service. She embodies the spirit of the luminaries who inspired her, channelling their legacy through her actions and teachings. Through her books, art, and social initiatives, she continues to inspire a new generation to embark on their own journeys of self-discovery, resilience, and altruism.

Her commitment to social betterment, particularly her focus on uplifting underprivileged children, reflects a deep understanding of the transformative potential of education and personal development. By integrating her knowledge of psychology, her artistic sensibilities, and her healing practices, Dr. Bansal has developed a holistic approach to social work that addresses both the immediate needs and the long-term well-being of the communities she serves.

As an author, Dr. Minakshi's writings offer a blend of inspirational insights, practical wisdom, and reflective contemplations drawn from her extensive reading and life experiences. Her books serve as a guide for those seeking to navigate the complexities of life with grace, resilience, and purpose. Through her narratives, she extends an invitation to her readers to explore the depths of their own potential and to contribute meaningfully to the collective well-being of society.

In Dr. Minakshi Bansal, we find a remarkable synthesis of the artist, the scholar, the healer, and the social activist. Her life's work stands as a beacon of hope and a source of inspiration for individuals seeking to make a difference in the world. Her story is a compelling reminder of the power of individual action, rooted in compassion and driven by a profound commitment to the betterment of humanity. Dr. Minakshi's legacy is not just in the tangible outcomes of her efforts but in the enduring spirit of inquiry, empathy, and service that she embodies.

ʔʔʔ

# Preface

In a world that often feels relentless in its pace and demands, finding moments of tranquility and peace can be an elusive pursuit. The constant bombardment of stimuli, from the cacophony of city life to the digital deluge of information, leaves many of us feeling overwhelmed and stressed. It is in this context that I embarked on a journey to explore the profound power of sound to heal, soothe, and restore. This book is the culmination of that journey, a testament to the transformative potential of sonic serenity.

My own fascination with sound began at a young age. I grew up surrounded by music, with melodies filling our home and rhythm pulsing through my veins. I always felt a deep connection to music, sensing its ability to uplift my spirits and calm my anxieties. As I grew older, I began to explore the wider world of sound, discovering the soothing sounds of nature, the meditative tones of singing bowls, and the rhythmic beats of drumming circles. Through these experiences, I came to realize that sound was more than just a sensory pleasure; it was a powerful tool for well-being.

Intrigued by this realization, I delved deeper into the science and history of sound healing, exploring ancient traditions and modern research. I learned that sound is not merely a vibration that travels through the air, but a fundamental force that interacts with our bodies and minds on a cellular level. Different frequencies and rhythms can influence our brainwaves, heart rate, and even our immune system. Sound can calm our nervous systems, reduce stress hormones, and promote relaxation. It can also enhance creativity, focus, and cognitive function.

As I immersed myself in the world of sound healing, I began to experiment with different sonic modalities, incorporating them into my daily life. I created playlists of calming music and nature sounds, attended sound baths and sound healing concerts, and practiced sound meditation. The results were profound. I found myself feeling less stressed, more centered, and more connected to myself and the world around me. I slept better, my mood improved, and I felt a renewed sense of energy and vitality.

Inspired by my own experiences, I felt compelled to share this newfound knowledge and passion with others. This book is the culmination of that desire, a guide to harnessing the power of sound for stress relief and overall well-being. In this book, we will explore the science behind sound healing, delve into different sonic modalities, and discover practical ways to incorporate sound into our daily lives.

We will begin by unveiling the hidden healer within sound, understanding how it can harmonize our internal rhythms and promote a state of balance and coherence. We will then delve into the science of sound, exploring how sound waves interact with our bodies and minds, influencing our emotions, thoughts, and physiology.

Next, we will embark on a sonic journey through the natural world, discovering the calming power of nature's soundtrack. We will explore how the sounds of nature, such as the rustling of leaves, the crashing of waves, or the chirping of birds, can soothe our souls and reconnect us with the earth's primordial rhythms.

We will then delve into the therapeutic potential of music, exploring how different genres and styles can evoke a wide range of emotions and physiological responses. We will learn how to create personalized playlists that support our well-being and discover the power of music to heal, uplift, and inspire.

Beyond music and nature sounds, we will venture into the realm of therapeutic soundscapes, exploring practices such as sound baths, binaural beats, and isochronic tones. We will discover how these immersive and transformative experiences can promote deep relaxation, reduce stress, and enhance overall well-being.

Throughout this book, I will share practical tips and techniques for incorporating sound into your daily routine. From mindful listening practices to the creation of peaceful sonic spaces in your home, you will discover a variety of ways to harness the power of sound to enhance your life.

In this book, I have also included inspiring stories of individuals who have experienced profound transformations through sound healing. Their stories are a testament to the power of sound to heal, inspire, and connect us on a deep level.

It is my hope that this book will serve as a guide and inspiration for your own sonic journey. May it empower you to take charge of your well-being, discover the sounds that resonate with your soul, and create a life filled with peace, harmony, and joy. Remember, the power to heal and transform is within you, and sound is a powerful ally in that journey.

*Dr. Minakshi Bansal*
*Social Activist*
*Ahmedabad, Gujarat, Bharat*

ᐳᐳᐳ

# ONE

## THE POWER OF SOUND: UNVEILING THE HIDDEN HEALER

Sound, in its simplest form, is a vibration that travels through the air and reaches our ears. Yet, it is far more than just a sensory experience. It's a primal force that has shaped our evolution, influenced our cultures, and holds the potential to profoundly affect our well-being. Throughout history, sound has been used for healing, from ancient chanting and drumming rituals to the modern practices of music therapy and sound baths. As we delve deeper into the science of sound, we are uncovering its remarkable capacity to soothe our souls, ease our minds, and restore our bodies.

The human body is a symphony of vibrations, with each cell, organ, and system resonating at a unique frequency. When we are exposed to harmonious sounds, our internal rhythms align, creating a state of balance and coherence. This is why the gentle lull of a mother's voice can calm a crying baby, the rhythmic beat of a drum can induce trance-like states, and the soothing melodies of classical music can lower blood pressure and heart rate.

Beyond its physiological effects, sound has a profound impact on our emotions and mental state. Music, in particular, can evoke a wide range of feelings, from joy and excitement to sadness and nostalgia. It can transport us to different times and places, awaken forgotten memories, and provide comfort in times of distress. The therapeutic use of music has been shown to reduce anxiety, depression, and pain, as well as improve mood, sleep, and cognitive function.

But the healing power of sound extends far beyond music. Natural sounds, such as the rustling of leaves, the crashing of waves, or the chirping of birds, have an innate ability to calm our nervous systems and connect us to the natural world. These sounds are often rich in calming frequencies, such as alpha and theta brainwaves, which promote relaxation and reduce stress. Spending time in nature and immersing ourselves in its sonic landscapes can be a powerful antidote to the noise and chaos of modern life.

Sound baths, a relatively new form of sound therapy, offer a unique way to experience the therapeutic benefits of sound. During a sound bath, participants lie down or sit comfortably while a practitioner plays a variety of instruments, such as singing bowls, gongs, chimes, and drums. The vibrations produced by these instruments wash over the body, creating a deeply relaxing and meditative state. Sound baths have been reported to reduce pain, anxiety, and insomnia, as well as promote deep relaxation, clarity, and emotional release.

Modern technology has also harnessed the power of sound for healing purposes. Binaural beats and isochronic tones, which are specific frequencies of sound, can entrain brainwave patterns and induce different states of consciousness. These technologies have been used to improve focus, enhance creativity, promote relaxation, and even alleviate symptoms of ADHD and anxiety.

The beauty of sound healing lies in its accessibility and versatility. It can be incorporated into our daily lives in countless ways, from listening to calming music while commuting to practicing sound meditation before bed. We can create sonic sanctuaries in our homes by using white noise machines, diffusers, or simply opening our windows to the sounds of nature. We can attend sound baths or sound healing concerts, or explore the vast array of sound therapy apps and online resources available.

The key is to find the sounds that resonate with us most deeply. Each individual has unique preferences and sensitivities to sound, so it's important to experiment and discover what works best for you. Whether it's the gentle strumming of a guitar, the rhythmic pulse of a drum, or the soothing tones of a singing bowl, the power of sound to heal is within our reach.

As we continue to explore the intricate relationship between sound and well-being, we are only beginning to scratch the surface of its potential. The emerging field of sound therapy is rapidly expanding, with new research and innovative applications constantly emerging. From personalized sound prescriptions to virtual reality sound experiences, the future of sound healing holds endless possibilities.

The power of sound is a hidden healer, waiting to be unleashed. By tuning into the vibrations that surround us and embracing the therapeutic potential of sound, we can unlock a deeper level of well-being, harmony, and inner peace.

ppp

*Sound is more than just noise; it is a symphony of vibrations that dance through our being, touching our hearts and souls. By embracing the power of sound, we unlock a hidden language of healing and transformation. In every note, a whisper of serenity awaits.*

# TWO

# SOUND & THE SENSES: A SYMPHONY FOR YOUR NERVOUS SYSTEM

Our senses are the gateways through which we experience the world around us, and sound plays a pivotal role in this intricate sensory symphony. Far from being merely a source of auditory pleasure, sound has a profound impact on our nervous system, shaping our emotions, influencing our behaviors, and even impacting our physical health. The relationship between sound and our senses is a fascinating dance, where vibrations transform into sensations, perceptions, and ultimately, experiences.

The journey of sound begins with its capture by our ears, intricate organs designed to translate vibrations in the air into electrical signals that our brains can interpret. As sound waves enter the ear canal, they cause the eardrum to vibrate, setting off a chain reaction that involves the tiny bones of the middle ear and the delicate hair cells of the inner ear. These hair cells, acting like miniature sensors, convert the vibrations into electrical impulses, which are then transmitted along the auditory nerve to the brain.

The brain, the conductor of our sensory orchestra, is where the magic truly happens. It is here that the raw data of sound is transformed into the rich tapestry of our auditory experience. Different regions of the brain are responsible for various aspects of sound perception, from identifying the pitch and timbre of a musical note to recognizing the familiar voice of a loved one. The brain's ability to process and interpret sound is nothing short of remarkable, allowing us to navigate our environment, communicate with others, and derive pleasure from music and other sonic delights.

However, the impact of sound on our nervous system extends far beyond the realm of auditory perception. Sound has a direct and often immediate effect on our emotions and physiological state. Consider the chills that run down your spine when you hear a soaring melody, the adrenaline rush triggered by the roar of a crowd, or the deep relaxation induced by the gentle lapping of waves. These emotional and physiological responses are mediated by the autonomic nervous system, the part of our nervous system that regulates involuntary bodily functions such as heart rate, breathing, and digestion.

Sound can activate both branches of the autonomic nervous system: the sympathetic nervous system, responsible for the "fight-or-flight" response, and the parasympathetic nervous system, responsible for the "rest-and-digest" response. Loud, jarring, or unpredictable sounds can trigger the sympathetic nervous system, leading to increased heart rate, rapid breathing, and heightened alertness. Conversely, soft, soothing, or rhythmic sounds can activate the parasympathetic nervous system, promoting relaxation, slowing down the heart rate, and facilitating digestion.

The ability of sound to modulate the autonomic nervous system has profound implications for our well-being. Chronic stress, a hallmark of modern life, can lead to a state of sympathetic overdrive, where the body is constantly in a state of high alert. This can have detrimental effects on our physical and mental health, increasing the risk of cardiovascular disease, anxiety, depression, and other chronic conditions. Sound-based interventions, such as music therapy, sound baths, and nature sounds, offer a promising avenue for counteracting the effects of stress and promoting relaxation.

Furthermore, sound can influence our brainwaves, the electrical patterns that reflect our mental state. Different brainwave frequencies are associated with various states of consciousness, from deep sleep (delta waves) to focused attention (beta waves). Certain types of sound, such as binaural beats and isochronic tones, can entrain brainwave patterns, essentially nudging the brain into a desired state. This phenomenon has been harnessed for therapeutic purposes, with sound-based interventions used to improve sleep, reduce anxiety, and enhance cognitive function.

The intricate relationship between sound and our senses is a testament to the interconnectedness of our mind and body. The vibrations that we perceive as sound not only stimulate our auditory system but also ripple through our entire being, influencing our emotions, physiology, and even our thoughts. By understanding how sound affects our nervous system, we can harness its power for our own well-being, using it to create a symphony of relaxation, focus, and inner peace.

ᐁᐁᐁ

*Nature's soundtrack, a symphony of whispers and rhythms, offers solace to the weary soul. Let the rustling leaves, the crashing waves, and the chirping birds transport you to a tranquil oasis, where stress melts away and peace reigns supreme.*

# THREE

# STRESS: THE SILENT SABOTEUR: UNDERSTANDING THE IMPACT ON BODY & MIND

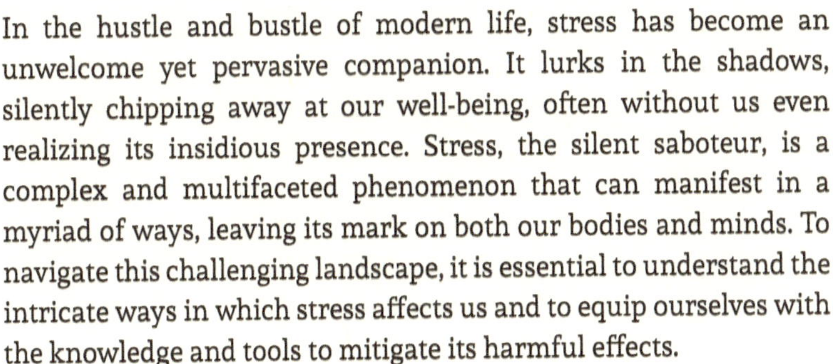

In the hustle and bustle of modern life, stress has become an unwelcome yet pervasive companion. It lurks in the shadows, silently chipping away at our well-being, often without us even realizing its insidious presence. Stress, the silent saboteur, is a complex and multifaceted phenomenon that can manifest in a myriad of ways, leaving its mark on both our bodies and minds. To navigate this challenging landscape, it is essential to understand the intricate ways in which stress affects us and to equip ourselves with the knowledge and tools to mitigate its harmful effects.

At its core, stress is a biological response to perceived threats or demands. When faced with a challenge, our bodies release a surge of hormones, such as cortisol and adrenaline, which prepare us to either fight or flee. This "fight-or-flight" response is an ancient survival mechanism that served our ancestors well in the face of immediate danger. However, in today's world, where stressors are often chronic and psychological rather than physical, this response can become maladaptive, leading to a cascade of negative consequences for our health.

The impact of stress on the body is far-reaching and profound. Chronic stress can weaken the immune system, making us more susceptible to infections and illnesses. It can disrupt hormonal balance, leading to menstrual irregularities, fertility problems, and thyroid dysfunction. Stress can also wreak havoc on the digestive system, causing symptoms such as stomach pain, bloating, diarrhea, and constipation. It can even accelerate the aging process, contributing to wrinkles, gray hair, and other signs of wear and tear.

But the effects of stress are not limited to the physical realm. Stress can also take a heavy toll on our mental and emotional well-being. Chronic stress can lead to anxiety, depression, irritability, and difficulty concentrating. It can impair memory and decision-making abilities, and even contribute to the development of more serious mental health disorders, such as post-traumatic stress disorder (PTSD). Stress can also disrupt sleep patterns, leading to insomnia and fatigue, which further exacerbate its negative effects.

The relationship between stress and the mind is a complex one, with a multitude of factors influencing how we perceive and respond to stressors. Our individual personalities, past experiences, and coping mechanisms all play a role in how we handle stress. Some individuals are naturally more resilient and able to bounce back from adversity, while others may be more vulnerable to the negative effects of stress. However, regardless of our individual differences, chronic stress can erode our resilience over time, leaving us feeling overwhelmed, exhausted, and emotionally drained.

One of the most insidious aspects of stress is its ability to become a self-perpetuating cycle. When we are stressed, we may engage in unhealthy behaviors, such as overeating, smoking, or excessive alcohol consumption, in an attempt to cope with our feelings. However, these behaviors only serve to exacerbate the problem, creating a vicious cycle of stress, unhealthy coping, and further stress. This is why it is crucial to develop healthy coping mechanisms for managing stress, such as exercise, meditation, spending time in nature, or seeking social support.

Understanding the impact of stress on our bodies and minds is the first step towards reclaiming our well-being. By recognizing the signs and symptoms of stress, we can take proactive measures to manage it before it takes a toll on our health. This may involve making lifestyle changes, such as prioritizing sleep, eating a healthy diet, and engaging in regular physical activity. It may also involve seeking professional help, such as therapy or counseling, to develop effective coping strategies and address any underlying emotional issues.

Stress is a silent saboteur, but it does not have to control our lives. By understanding its impact and taking steps to manage it, we can break free from its grasp and cultivate a life of balance, resilience, and well-being. Remember, stress is a normal part of life, but it is how we respond to it that ultimately determines its effect on our health and happiness. By prioritizing self-care, seeking support when needed, and developing healthy coping mechanisms, we can transform stress from a silent saboteur into a catalyst for growth and resilience.

ppp

*Music, a universal language that transcends boundaries, speaks directly to the heart. Let its melodies soothe your soul, its rhythms invigorate your spirit, and its harmonies create a tapestry of joy and well-being.*

# FOUR

# SONIC SCIENCE: HOW SOUND WAVES INFLUENCE YOUR WELL-BEING

The world around us is alive with sound, a symphony of vibrations that dance through the air and penetrate our very being. These vibrations, known as sound waves, hold a remarkable power to influence our well-being, shaping our emotions, physiology, and even our consciousness. Delving into the science of sound reveals a captivating interplay between physics, biology, and psychology, illuminating how these seemingly intangible waves can profoundly affect our lives.

At its core, sound is a form of energy that travels through a medium, such as air or water, as a series of compressions and rarefactions. These fluctuations in pressure create waves that propagate outward from the source, much like ripples in a pond. The characteristics of these waves, such as their frequency (pitch), amplitude (loudness), and timbre (tone color), determine the unique qualities of the sound we perceive.

Our ears, finely tuned instruments of perception, are exquisitely adapted to capture and interpret these sound waves. The outer ear funnels the waves into the ear canal, where they cause the eardrum to vibrate. This vibration is then transmitted to the middle ear, where tiny bones amplify the signal and pass it on to the inner ear. Here, within the cochlea, a snail-shaped structure filled with fluid, the true magic of hearing occurs. Thousands of tiny hair cells lining the cochlea sway in response to the vibrations, converting them into electrical impulses that are sent along the auditory nerve to the brain.

The brain, the command center of our nervous system, is where the raw data of sound is transformed into the rich tapestry of our auditory experience. Different regions of the brain are responsible for various aspects of sound processing, from discerning the direction and distance of a sound source to recognizing familiar voices and melodies. The brain's ability to analyze and interpret sound is nothing short of extraordinary, allowing us to navigate our environment, communicate with others, and derive pleasure from music and other sonic delights.

However, the influence of sound extends far beyond the realm of auditory perception. Sound waves interact with our bodies on a cellular level, influencing our physiology in surprising ways. Research has shown that specific frequencies of sound can alter heart rate, respiration, blood pressure, and even brainwave patterns. This phenomenon, known as entrainment, occurs when our bodies synchronize with external rhythms, such as the beat of a drum or the pulse of a melody.

Sound can also trigger the release of neurotransmitters, the chemical messengers that regulate our mood, emotions, and cognitive function. For example, listening to calming music can increase the production of dopamine, a neurotransmitter associated with pleasure and reward, while reducing the levels of cortisol, a stress hormone. This explains why music can have such a profound impact on our emotional state, lifting our spirits, easing anxiety, and even alleviating pain.

Moreover, sound has been shown to influence our cognitive abilities, affecting our attention, memory, and creativity. Studies have found that listening to certain types of music, such as classical or ambient music, can improve focus and concentration, while other genres, such as upbeat or rhythmic music, can enhance motivation and creativity. The use of sound in educational settings has also been explored, with promising results suggesting that sound can enhance learning and memory recall.

The therapeutic potential of sound is vast and varied. Sound therapy, a burgeoning field of complementary medicine, utilizes various techniques to harness the healing power of sound. These techniques may include listening to specific frequencies of sound, using sound baths or vibrational instruments, or participating in guided meditations that incorporate sound. Sound therapy has been shown to reduce stress, anxiety, and pain, as well as improve sleep, mood, and overall well-being.

The science of sound is a captivating journey that reveals the intricate ways in which sound waves influence our lives. From the mechanics of hearing to the profound effects on our emotions, physiology, and cognition, sound is a force to be reckoned with. By understanding the science behind sound, we can tap into its vast potential for healing, growth, and transformation, creating a symphony of well-being that resonates with our very soul.

ᐅᐅᐅ

*In the stillness of a sound bath, let the vibrations wash over you, releasing tension and restoring balance. Like a gentle wave, sound can cleanse your energy, leaving you feeling refreshed and renewed.*

# FIVE

# Nature's Soundtrack: Harnessing the Calming Power of Natural Sounds

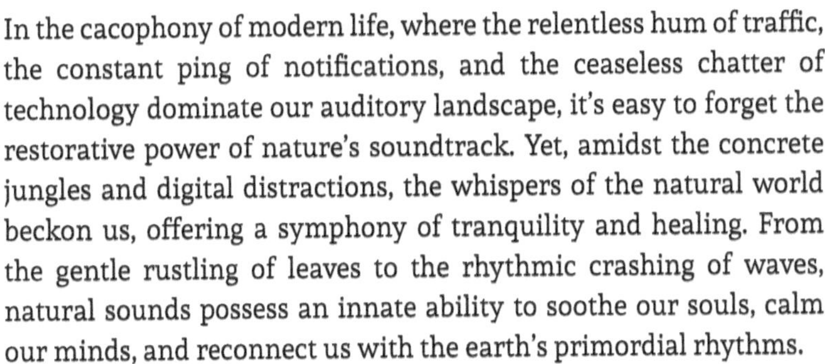

In the cacophony of modern life, where the relentless hum of traffic, the constant ping of notifications, and the ceaseless chatter of technology dominate our auditory landscape, it's easy to forget the restorative power of nature's soundtrack. Yet, amidst the concrete jungles and digital distractions, the whispers of the natural world beckon us, offering a symphony of tranquility and healing. From the gentle rustling of leaves to the rhythmic crashing of waves, natural sounds possess an innate ability to soothe our souls, calm our minds, and reconnect us with the earth's primordial rhythms.

Throughout human history, nature has been our constant companion, providing sustenance, shelter, and inspiration. Our ancestors lived in close communion with the natural world, attuned to its cycles and rhythms. The sounds of nature were not mere background noise but an integral part of their daily lives, weaving a tapestry of comfort and familiarity. As we have moved further away from nature, immersing ourselves in artificial environments and synthetic sounds, we have lost touch with this ancient connection.

The sounds of nature are more than just pleasant auditory experiences. They are a complex symphony of frequencies, rhythms, and patterns that resonate with our very being. Research has shown that exposure to natural sounds can have a profound impact on our physiological and psychological well-being. It can lower blood pressure, reduce heart rate, and decrease levels of stress hormones such as cortisol. It can also improve mood, boost creativity, and enhance cognitive function.

One of the key ways in which natural sounds exert their calming influence is through their ability to entrain our brainwaves. Brainwaves are the electrical patterns that reflect our mental state. Different brainwave frequencies are associated with different states of consciousness, from deep sleep (delta waves) to focused attention (beta waves). Natural sounds, with their gentle rhythms and soothing frequencies, can help to shift our brainwaves into a more relaxed and meditative state, promoting feelings of tranquility and well-being.

The rhythmic patterns found in nature, such as the ebb and flow of ocean waves or the gentle patter of rain, can also induce a state of deep relaxation known as the "alpha state." This state is characterized by increased creativity, improved focus, and reduced anxiety. It is often associated with meditation and other mindfulness practices, and is believed to be a key factor in the restorative effects of spending time in nature.

Beyond their physiological and psychological benefits, natural sounds also have a profound impact on our emotional well-being.

The sounds of nature can evoke feelings of awe, wonder, and connection to something larger than ourselves. They can remind us of our place in the web of life, and help us to feel more grounded and centered. This sense of connection to nature can be especially important in times of stress or adversity, providing a source of comfort and resilience.

The healing power of natural sounds is not limited to a specific type of sound or environment. Whether it's the gentle chirping of birds in a forest, the rhythmic crashing of waves on a beach, or the soothing trickle of a mountain stream, each natural sound has its own unique therapeutic qualities. The key is to find the sounds that resonate with you most deeply and to incorporate them into your daily life.

In today's fast-paced world, it can be challenging to find time to immerse ourselves in nature. However, even brief exposures to natural sounds can have a significant impact on our well-being. Listening to recordings of nature sounds, spending time in a park or garden, or simply opening a window to the sounds of the outdoors can all be effective ways to reap the benefits of nature's soundtrack.

As we become more aware of the detrimental effects of noise pollution and the importance of auditory well-being, the use of natural sounds for therapeutic purposes is gaining momentum. Sound therapists, environmental psychologists, and even architects are increasingly incorporating natural sounds into their practices, recognizing their potential to create more peaceful and restorative environments.

Nature's soundtrack is a gift, a symphony of healing that has been playing for millennia. By tuning in to its melodies and rhythms, we can tap into a profound source of well-being, reconnecting with our roots and restoring balance to our lives. In a world that is constantly bombarding us with noise and distractions, the sounds of nature offer a sanctuary of peace, a reminder of the beauty and harmony that exist within and around us. Let us not forget the power of this ancient music, for it holds the key to unlocking a deeper level of tranquility and wholeness.

♭♭♭

*Binaural beats and isochronic tones, whispers of frequency, can guide your mind into a state of deep relaxation. Allow these rhythmic patterns to entrain your brainwaves, unlocking the door to tranquility and inner peace.*

# SIX

# MUSIC AS MEDICINE: FINDING YOUR PERSONAL STRESS-RELIEF PLAYLIST

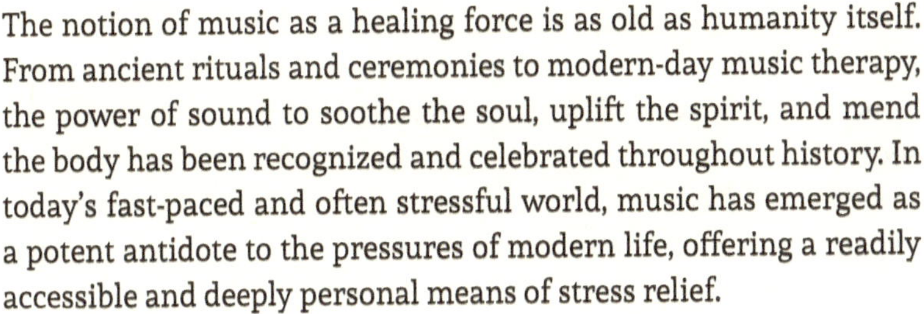

The notion of music as a healing force is as old as humanity itself. From ancient rituals and ceremonies to modern-day music therapy, the power of sound to soothe the soul, uplift the spirit, and mend the body has been recognized and celebrated throughout history. In today's fast-paced and often stressful world, music has emerged as a potent antidote to the pressures of modern life, offering a readily accessible and deeply personal means of stress relief.

Music's impact on our well-being is not merely anecdotal or subjective; it is backed by a growing body of scientific evidence. Research has shown that listening to music can reduce anxiety, lower blood pressure, and even boost the immune system. Music has also been found to improve mood, enhance cognitive function, and promote relaxation. The therapeutic benefits of music are so well-documented that it is now used in a variety of clinical settings, from hospitals and rehabilitation centers to mental health clinics and hospices.

The science behind music's healing power is complex and multifaceted. Music activates multiple regions of the brain, including those responsible for emotions, memory, and movement. It can stimulate the release of dopamine, a neurotransmitter associated with pleasure and reward, and reduce the levels of cortisol, a stress hormone. Music can also entrain brainwave patterns, inducing a state of deep relaxation and calmness.

But music's power goes beyond its physiological effects. It has a unique ability to connect with us on an emotional level, evoking memories, feelings, and associations that can be both comforting and cathartic. Music can transport us to different times and places, allowing us to relive cherished moments or escape from the pressures of the present. It can also provide a safe space for expressing and processing difficult emotions, such as grief, anger, or fear.

Finding your personal stress-relief playlist is a deeply personal journey. There is no one-size-fits-all approach, as different types of music resonate with different people. Some may find solace in the soothing sounds of classical or ambient music, while others may prefer the upbeat rhythms of pop or dance music. The key is to experiment and discover the genres and artists that resonate with you most deeply.

When creating your stress-relief playlist, consider the mood you want to cultivate. If you're feeling anxious or overwhelmed, you may want to choose music with a slower tempo and calming melodies. If you're feeling down or lethargic, you may want to opt for more upbeat and energetic music. Pay attention to how different types of music make you feel, and don't be afraid to experiment with different genres and artists.

Your stress-relief playlist should be a dynamic and evolving collection of songs that reflect your changing needs and moods. Don't be afraid to add new songs or remove old ones as your preferences change. The most important thing is that your playlist is a source of comfort and inspiration, a sonic sanctuary where you can escape from the stresses of daily life and recharge your batteries.

Here are some tips for creating your personal stress-relief playlist:

Start with a few songs you already know and love. These can be songs that have always had a calming or uplifting effect on you.

Explore different genres and artists. Don't limit yourself to the music you usually listen to. Branch out and try new things. You may be surprised at what you discover.

Pay attention to the tempo and rhythm of the music. Slower tempos and gentle rhythms are generally more relaxing, while faster tempos and more complex rhythms can be more energizing.

Consider the lyrics. If you're choosing music with lyrics, make sure the words are positive and uplifting. Avoid songs that are sad, angry, or aggressive.

Create a variety of playlists for different moods and situations. You may want a playlist for when you're feeling stressed, another for when you're feeling down, and another for when you need to focus or relax.

Listen to your playlist regularly. The more you listen to your playlist, the more effective it will become at reducing stress. Make it a part of your daily routine, whether it's during your commute, while you're working, or before bed.

Music is a powerful tool for healing and self-care. By creating a personal stress-relief playlist, you can harness the power of music to soothe your soul, uplift your spirit, and restore your well-being. So go ahead and create your own sonic sanctuary – your mind and body will thank you for it.

ᐅᐅᐅ

*The breath, a rhythmic dance of life, holds the key to unlocking inner peace. Through conscious breathing, we can harmonize our bodies and minds, creating a symphony of relaxation and well-being.*

# SEVEN

# BEYOND MUSIC: EXPLORING THE THERAPEUTIC SOUNDSCAPES OF SOUND BATHS & BEYOND

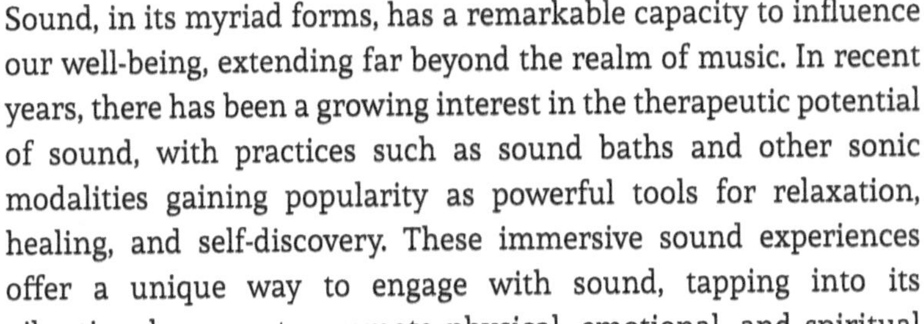

Sound, in its myriad forms, has a remarkable capacity to influence our well-being, extending far beyond the realm of music. In recent years, there has been a growing interest in the therapeutic potential of sound, with practices such as sound baths and other sonic modalities gaining popularity as powerful tools for relaxation, healing, and self-discovery. These immersive sound experiences offer a unique way to engage with sound, tapping into its vibrational energy to promote physical, emotional, and spiritual well-being.

Sound baths, in particular, have emerged as a popular form of sound therapy, attracting individuals seeking relief from stress, anxiety, and other ailments. During a sound bath, participants typically lie down or sit comfortably in a quiet space while a practitioner plays a variety of instruments, such as singing bowls, gongs, chimes, and drums. These instruments produce rich, resonant tones that wash over the body, creating a deeply relaxing and meditative state.

The science behind sound baths is rooted in the understanding that sound is a form of vibration that can affect our physical and energetic bodies. Sound waves travel through our bodies, interacting with our cells, tissues, and organs. This interaction can trigger a cascade of physiological responses, including the release of endorphins, the body's natural painkillers, and the activation of the parasympathetic nervous system, responsible for rest and relaxation.

The effects of a sound bath can be profound and varied. Many participants report feeling deeply relaxed and rejuvenated, with a sense of peace and well-being that can last for days. Sound baths have also been shown to reduce stress, anxiety, and pain, as well as improve sleep, mood, and overall well-being. Some individuals even report experiencing altered states of consciousness, such as heightened awareness, clarity, and spiritual connection.

But sound baths are just one aspect of the vast landscape of therapeutic sound. There are many other sonic modalities that can be used to promote healing and well-being. For example, tuning forks, which produce pure tones at specific frequencies, can be used to stimulate acupuncture points and balance energy flow in the body.

Chanting and toning, which involve vocalizing specific sounds or mantras, can create vibrations that resonate with different parts of the body, promoting relaxation and healing. Even the simple act of listening to nature sounds, such as the rustling of leaves or the flowing of water, can have a profound calming effect on our nervous systems.

The therapeutic potential of sound lies in its ability to bypass the analytical mind and access deeper levels of consciousness. Unlike traditional talk therapy, which relies on language and cognitive processes, sound therapy works on a more primal level, bypassing the need for words and explanations.

This makes it particularly effective for individuals who struggle with verbal communication or who have experienced trauma.

Moreover, sound therapy is a holistic approach to healing, addressing the mind, body, and spirit as interconnected aspects of our being. It recognizes that dis-ease can manifest on multiple levels, and seeks to restore balance and harmony to the entire system.

This is why sound therapy is often used in conjunction with other healing modalities, such as massage, acupuncture, and energy work.

As our understanding of the therapeutic potential of sound continues to evolve, we are discovering new and innovative ways to harness its power for healing.

Researchers are exploring the use of sound in the treatment of a wide range of conditions, from chronic pain and PTSD to dementia and autism. Sound is also being used to enhance performance, creativity, and overall well-being.

While the science of sound therapy is still in its infancy, the anecdotal evidence and growing body of research suggest that sound has a profound capacity to heal and transform. Whether through sound baths, tuning forks, chanting, or simply listening to nature sounds, sound therapy offers a safe, accessible, and effective way to promote well-being and tap into our innate healing potential.

As we continue to explore the vast and complex world of sound, we are only beginning to uncover its limitless possibilities for healing and transformation.

 PPP

*Your home, a sanctuary of peace, can be enhanced by the gentle touch of sound. Let the soothing melodies of nature or the calming hum of a white noise machine create an oasis of tranquility where you can truly unwind and recharge.*

# EIGHT

# THE RHYTHM OF RELAXATION: USING BINAURAL BEATS & ISOCHRONIC TONES

In the pursuit of tranquility and well-being, we often find ourselves drawn to the soothing embrace of sound. Beyond the melodic harmonies of music lies a realm of auditory frequencies that hold the potential to deeply influence our mental and physical states. Binaural beats and isochronic tones, two distinct yet related phenomena, have emerged as powerful tools for promoting relaxation, focus, and even altered states of consciousness.

These rhythmic patterns of sound, when listened to through headphones, can entrain our brainwaves, nudging them into specific frequencies associated with different states of mind.

Binaural beats are created by presenting two slightly different frequencies of sound, one to each ear. The brain perceives the difference between these two frequencies as a third, phantom beat, known as the binaural beat. This beat, which is not actually present in the external sound, is believed to induce a state of brainwave entrainment, where the brain's electrical activity begins to synchronize with the frequency of the binaural beat.

Isochronic tones, on the other hand, are single tones that are pulsed on and off at regular intervals, creating a rhythmic beat. While they do not require headphones to be effective, they are generally considered to be more potent when listened to through headphones, as the sound is more isolated and focused. Like binaural beats, isochronic tones can also induce brainwave entrainment, leading to changes in mental and physical states.

The concept of brainwave entrainment is based on the idea that our brains naturally synchronize with external rhythms. This phenomenon is evident in everyday life, such as when we tap our feet to the beat of a song or feel our heart rate synchronize with the rhythm of a drum.

By deliberately introducing specific frequencies of sound through binaural beats or isochronic tones, we can harness this natural tendency to shift our brainwaves into desired states.

Different frequencies of brainwaves are associated with different states of consciousness. For example, delta waves (0.5-4 Hz) are associated with deep sleep, theta waves (4-8 Hz) with relaxation and meditation, alpha waves (8-12 Hz) with calm focus and creativity, and beta waves (12-38 Hz) with alertness and concentration.

By listening to binaural beats or isochronic tones that correspond to specific frequencies, we can encourage our brains to enter these desired states.

For example, if we want to relax and de-stress, we can listen to binaural beats or isochronic tones in the alpha or theta range. This can help to reduce anxiety, promote calmness, and improve sleep quality. If we want to enhance focus and concentration, we can listen to frequencies in the beta range. This can help to improve cognitive function, boost productivity, and sharpen mental clarity.

The potential benefits of binaural beats and isochronic tones extend beyond relaxation and focus. They have also been explored for their potential to alleviate pain, reduce anxiety and depression, and even enhance creativity. Some studies have even suggested that they may have a role to play in the treatment of certain neurological conditions, such as ADHD and epilepsy.

However, it is important to note that the research on binaural beats and isochronic tones is still in its early stages, and more studies are needed to fully understand their effects and potential applications.

It is also important to use these tools with caution, as they can have unintended consequences if not used properly. For example, listening to binaural beats or isochronic tones at high volumes or for extended periods of time can cause headaches, dizziness, or nausea.

When using binaural beats or isochronic tones, it is important to start with short listening sessions and gradually increase the duration as tolerated. It is also important to choose frequencies that are appropriate for your desired state of mind.

If you are unsure which frequencies to use, it is always best to consult with a qualified practitioner.

Binaural beats and isochronic tones are powerful tools that can be used to promote relaxation, focus, and well-being. However, it is important to use them responsibly and with caution.

By understanding the science behind these rhythmic patterns of sound, we can harness their potential to unlock new levels of inner peace, creativity, and overall health.

❧❧❧

*Technology, when harnessed with intention, can be a powerful tool for well-being. Explore the sonic landscape of apps and devices, discovering new ways to tap into the healing power of sound and create a personalized oasis of serenity.*

# NINE

# Finding Your Frequency: Discovering the Sounds that Soothe You Most

In the vast symphony of sounds that surround us, each individual possesses a unique sonic fingerprint, a collection of frequencies and rhythms that resonate with our very being. These sounds, when discovered and embraced, have the power to unlock a deep sense of calm, joy, and well-being. Finding your frequency is a journey of self-discovery, a quest to uncover the sounds that soothe your soul, calm your mind, and nourish your spirit.

The concept of frequency, in the context of sound, refers to the number of vibrations per second that a sound wave produces. Different frequencies create different pitches, from the low rumble of a bass drum to the high-pitched trill of a piccolo.

Our bodies are innately attuned to these frequencies, with each organ and system resonating at its own unique rhythm. When we are exposed to sounds that harmonize with our internal frequencies, we experience a sense of resonance, a feeling of alignment and balance.

The quest to find your frequency is not a one-size-fits-all endeavor. It is a deeply personal exploration, as each individual's sonic preferences are as unique as their fingerprints.

What soothes one person may irritate another, and what brings joy to one may leave another feeling indifferent. The key is to listen to your body, your emotions, and your intuition as you explore the vast landscape of sound.

One way to begin your journey is to pay attention to the sounds that naturally draw you in. Do you find yourself captivated by the gentle lapping of waves, the rustling of leaves in the wind, or the chirping of birds?

Do you feel a sense of calm and serenity when you listen to classical music, ambient soundscapes, or nature recordings? These are all clues that can guide you towards your personal frequency.

Experimentation is key in this process. Try listening to different types of music, nature sounds, and other sonic modalities. Pay attention to how each sound makes you feel. Does it evoke feelings of joy, relaxation, or inspiration? Does it make you feel agitated, anxious, or bored? Trust your instincts and gravitate towards the sounds that resonate with you on a deep level.

As you explore different sounds, you may notice that certain frequencies or rhythms have a particularly profound effect on you. Some people find that low-frequency sounds, such as the rumble of a drum or the hum of a Tibetan singing bowl, create a sense of grounding and stability.

Others may prefer high-frequency sounds, such as the tinkling of chimes or the singing of crystal bowls, which can promote a feeling of lightness and expansion.

The rhythm of sound can also be a significant factor in determining its effect on our well-being. Slow, steady rhythms can induce a state of deep relaxation, while faster, more complex rhythms can be energizing and uplifting.

Some people find that binaural beats or isochronic tones, which are specific frequencies of sound that can entrain brainwaves, are particularly effective for promoting relaxation, focus, or creativity.

Finding your frequency is not just about discovering the sounds that soothe you in the moment. It is also about understanding how sound can be used as a tool for long-term well-being. Incorporating sound into your daily routine, whether through listening to music, practicing sound meditation, or attending sound baths, can have a cumulative effect on your overall health and happiness.

Sound can be a powerful ally in managing stress, anxiety, and other emotional challenges. It can help to calm the nervous system, reduce tension, and promote feelings of peace and well-being. Sound can also be used to enhance focus, creativity, and productivity, as well as to improve sleep and boost the immune system.

The journey to find your frequency is an ongoing one. Our sonic preferences may change over time as we grow and evolve. It is important to remain open to new sounds and experiences, and to continue exploring the vast and ever-changing landscape of sound.

Ultimately, finding your frequency is about discovering the sounds that nourish your soul and help you to live a more vibrant and fulfilling life. It is about connecting with the universal language of sound and using it to unlock your full potential.

So go ahead and explore, experiment, and discover the symphony of sounds that resonate with your unique being. The journey to finding your frequency is a rewarding one, and the rewards are immeasurable.

ﾚﾚﾚ

*In the company of others, the power of sound multiplies. Let the shared experience of music, chanting, or simply listening to the sounds of nature forge connections, create community, and uplift your spirit.*

# TEN

# SONIC SELF-CARE RITUALS: INCORPORATING SOUND INTO YOUR DAILY ROUTINE

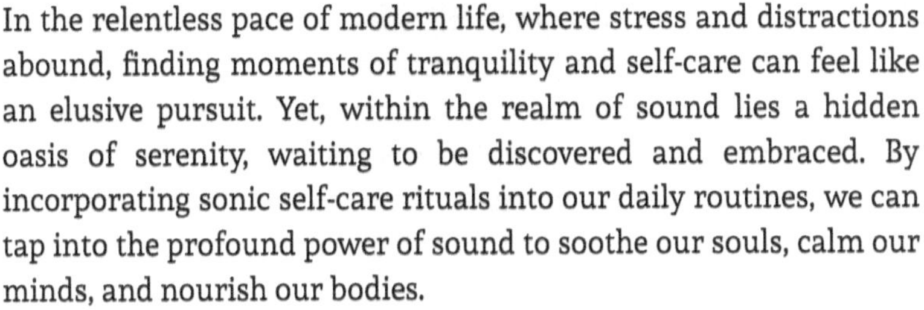

In the relentless pace of modern life, where stress and distractions abound, finding moments of tranquility and self-care can feel like an elusive pursuit. Yet, within the realm of sound lies a hidden oasis of serenity, waiting to be discovered and embraced. By incorporating sonic self-care rituals into our daily routines, we can tap into the profound power of sound to soothe our souls, calm our minds, and nourish our bodies.

Sound, in its myriad forms, has a remarkable capacity to influence our well-being. It can evoke a wide range of emotions, from joy and excitement to peace and tranquility. It can transport us to different times and places, awaken forgotten memories, and provide comfort in times of distress. By consciously incorporating sound into our daily lives, we can harness its therapeutic potential and create a sanctuary of serenity amidst the chaos.

The beauty of sonic self-care rituals is their versatility and adaptability. They can be tailored to fit seamlessly into our existing routines, requiring minimal effort and time commitment. Whether you are a busy professional, a stay-at-home parent, or a student juggling multiple responsibilities, there are countless ways to integrate sound into your day and reap its myriad benefits.

One of the simplest and most accessible sonic self-care rituals is to start your day with a mindful listening practice. Upon waking, instead of immediately reaching for your phone or rushing into your daily tasks, take a few moments to simply be present with the sounds around you. Listen to the chirping of birds, the rustling of leaves, or the gentle hum of your refrigerator.

Notice the subtle nuances of each sound, the rise and fall of its pitch, the texture of its timbre. This simple act of mindful listening can help to ground you in the present moment, clear your mind, and set a positive tone for the day ahead.

Throughout the day, you can incorporate sound into your routine in various ways. If you have a commute, use this time to listen to calming music or nature sounds. Create a playlist of your favorite songs that uplift your mood and inspire you. If you work in a noisy environment, consider using noise-canceling headphones or listening to white noise to create a more peaceful atmosphere.

During your lunch break, take a few minutes to step outside and immerse yourself in the sounds of nature. Notice the sounds of the wind in the trees, the chatter of squirrels, or the distant hum of traffic.

In the evening, as you wind down for the day, create a relaxing sonic ambiance in your home. Dim the lights, light some candles, and put on some soothing music or nature sounds. Take a warm bath with Epsom salts and essential oils, and let the sound of the water wash away your worries.

If you have trouble sleeping, try listening to binaural beats or isochronic tones, which can help to entrain your brainwaves into a state of deep relaxation.

The power of sound extends beyond the auditory realm. It can also be experienced through vibration. Sound healing modalities, such as singing bowls, tuning forks, and gongs, utilize the vibrational properties of sound to promote relaxation, healing, and spiritual connection.

These instruments produce rich, resonant tones that can be felt throughout the body, creating a deeply immersive and transformative experience.

Incorporating sonic self-care rituals into your daily routine can have a profound impact on your overall well-being. Sound can help to reduce stress, anxiety, and pain, as well as improve sleep, mood, and cognitive function.

It can also enhance creativity, boost productivity, and promote a sense of inner peace and harmony. By making sound a conscious part of your life, you can tap into its vast potential for healing and transformation.

The key to creating effective sonic self-care rituals is to experiment and find what works best for you. There is no one-size-fits-all approach, as everyone's sonic preferences are unique.

Some people may find that classical music soothes them, while others may prefer nature sounds or ambient music. The most important thing is to choose sounds that you find enjoyable and relaxing.

Sonic self-care rituals can be a powerful tool for cultivating well-being and resilience in the face of life's challenges. By incorporating sound into our daily routines, we can create a sanctuary of serenity amidst the chaos, nurture our bodies and minds, and connect with our deepest selves.

So go ahead and explore the vast and beautiful world of sound. Let it be your guide on a journey of self-discovery, healing, and transformation.

ᚦᚦᚦ

*The future of sound healing is a symphony of possibilities. As technology advances and our understanding of sound deepens, we are only beginning to scratch the surface of its potential to heal, transform, and elevate our lives.*

# ELEVEN

# SOUND FOR SLEEP: CREATING A TRANQUIL SLEEP SANCTUARY WITH SOUND

Sleep, a fundamental pillar of well-being, often eludes us in our modern, fast-paced lives. The pursuit of restful slumber has led many to explore various techniques and tools, and one often overlooked yet powerful ally is sound. Beyond its ability to entertain and communicate, sound possesses a unique capacity to influence our sleep patterns, soothe our minds, and create a tranquil sanctuary for rejuvenation. By harnessing the power of sound, we can unlock the door to deeper, more restful sleep and wake up feeling refreshed and revitalized.

The relationship between sound and sleep is deeply rooted in our biology. Our brains are constantly processing auditory information, even while we sleep. Sounds can either disrupt our sleep or lull us into a state of deep relaxation, depending on their nature and intensity. Understanding how different types of sounds affect our sleep can empower us to create a sonic environment that promotes optimal rest.

One of the most common challenges to sleep is noise pollution. The constant hum of traffic, the neighbor's barking dog, or the dripping faucet can all disrupt our sleep cycles and prevent us from entering the deeper stages of sleep where restoration truly occurs. Fortunately, sound can also be used to mask unwanted noises and create a more peaceful sleep environment.

White noise, pink noise, and brown noise are all examples of sound masking techniques that can be used to block out disruptive sounds and promote relaxation. White noise is a consistent sound that covers a wide range of frequencies, similar to the static on a radio. Pink noise has a deeper, more resonant quality, while brown noise is even deeper and more rumbling. These sounds can be generated by white noise machines, fans, or even smartphone apps, and have been shown to improve sleep quality by reducing the time it takes to fall asleep and increasing the amount of time spent in deep sleep.

Beyond sound masking, certain types of sounds can actively promote relaxation and sleepiness. Nature sounds, such as the gentle rustling of leaves, the rhythmic crashing of waves, or the soothing chirping of crickets, have been shown to have a calming effect on the nervous system, lowering heart rate and blood pressure. These sounds are often rich in calming frequencies, such as alpha and theta brainwaves, which are associated with relaxation and sleep.

Music can also be a powerful tool for promoting sleep. Slow, melodic music with a tempo of around 60 beats per minute has been found to be particularly effective for inducing sleepiness. This type of music can slow down the heart rate, breathing, and brainwave activity, creating a state of deep relaxation conducive to sleep.

Another emerging area of interest is the use of binaural beats and isochronic tones for sleep enhancement. Binaural beats are created by playing two slightly different frequencies of sound, one to each ear. The brain perceives the difference between these two frequencies as a third, phantom beat, known as the binaural beat. This beat, which is not actually present in the external sound, is believed to induce a state of brainwave entrainment, where the brain's electrical activity begins to synchronize with the frequency of the binaural beat.

Isochronic tones are similar to binaural beats, but they consist of single tones that are pulsed on and off at regular intervals. Like binaural beats, isochronic tones can also induce brainwave entrainment, leading to changes in mental and physical states. Both binaural beats and isochronic tones have been studied for their potential to improve sleep quality, reduce anxiety, and promote relaxation.

Creating a tranquil sleep sanctuary with sound involves more than just choosing the right sounds to listen to. It also involves creating a sleep-conducive environment that minimizes distractions and promotes relaxation. This includes keeping the bedroom cool, dark, and quiet, avoiding caffeine and alcohol before bed, and establishing a consistent sleep schedule.

The use of sound for sleep is a rapidly growing field, with new research and innovations emerging all the time. From smart speakers that play personalized soundscapes to wearable devices that track sleep patterns and deliver targeted sound therapy, the possibilities are endless. As we continue to explore the intricate relationship between sound and sleep, we are discovering new and exciting ways to harness the power of sound to unlock the secrets of restful slumber.

In a world that is constantly bombarding us with noise and distractions, the power of sound to create a tranquil sleep sanctuary is a gift. By incorporating sound into our sleep routines, we can transform our bedrooms into havens of peace and tranquility, where we can escape from the stresses of daily life and awaken feeling refreshed and rejuvenated. So let us embrace the soothing embrace of sound and rediscover the joy of restful sleep.

ppp

*Your sonic journey is unique and personal. Embrace the sounds that resonate with your soul, and let them guide you towards a life filled with peace, harmony, and joy.*

# TWELVE

# Sonic Solutions for Anxiety: Quieting the Anxious Mind

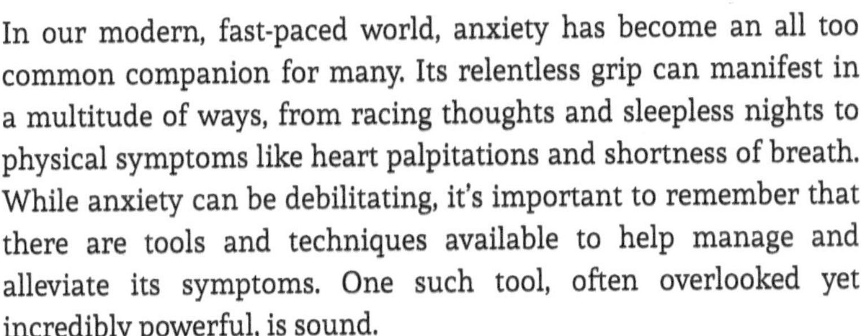

In our modern, fast-paced world, anxiety has become an all too common companion for many. Its relentless grip can manifest in a multitude of ways, from racing thoughts and sleepless nights to physical symptoms like heart palpitations and shortness of breath. While anxiety can be debilitating, it's important to remember that there are tools and techniques available to help manage and alleviate its symptoms. One such tool, often overlooked yet incredibly powerful, is sound.

Sound has a profound impact on our minds and bodies, influencing our emotions, thoughts, and physiological states. It can be a source of both stress and solace, depending on its nature and our individual responses. However, by intentionally utilizing specific types of sounds, we can harness their therapeutic potential to quiet the anxious mind, promote relaxation, and restore inner peace.

The science behind sound's ability to soothe anxiety is rooted in the intricate workings of our nervous system. When we experience anxiety, our sympathetic nervous system, responsible for the "fight-or-flight" response, becomes activated. This triggers a cascade of physiological changes, including increased heart rate, rapid breathing, and the release of stress hormones like cortisol. These changes prepare us to deal with perceived threats, but when anxiety becomes chronic, this heightened state of arousal can take a toll on our well-being.

Sound can counteract these effects by activating the parasympathetic nervous system, responsible for the "rest-and-digest" response. This branch of the nervous system helps to slow down the heart rate, regulate breathing, and promote relaxation. Certain types of sounds, such as slow, rhythmic music, nature sounds, or binaural beats, have been shown to stimulate the parasympathetic nervous system and induce a state of calmness.

Music, in particular, has a long history of being used to soothe the soul and ease the mind. Studies have shown that listening to calming music can reduce anxiety, lower blood pressure, and even boost the immune system. The tempo, rhythm, and melody of music can all influence its effect on our emotions. Slow, melodic music with a tempo of around 60 beats per minute has been found to be particularly effective for reducing anxiety and promoting relaxation.

Nature sounds, such as the gentle rustling of leaves, the rhythmic crashing of waves, or the soothing chirping of birds, can also be incredibly effective for calming the anxious mind. These sounds are often rich in calming frequencies, such as alpha and theta brainwaves, which are associated with relaxation and stress reduction. Spending time in nature or listening to recordings of nature sounds can be a powerful antidote to the noise and chaos of modern life.

Binaural beats and isochronic tones, which are specific frequencies of sound that can entrain brainwave patterns, offer another promising avenue for anxiety relief. These sounds, when listened to through headphones, can induce a state of deep relaxation and calmness by synchronizing brainwave activity with the desired frequency. While research on binaural beats and isochronic tones is still ongoing, preliminary studies suggest that they may be effective for reducing anxiety, improving sleep, and enhancing mood.

Sound baths, a relatively new form of sound therapy, have also gained popularity as a way to alleviate anxiety and promote relaxation. During a sound bath, participants lie down or sit comfortably in a quiet space while a practitioner plays a variety of instruments, such as singing bowls, gongs, chimes, and drums. The vibrations produced by these instruments wash over the body, creating a deeply relaxing and meditative state. Sound baths have been reported to reduce anxiety, stress, and pain, as well as improve sleep and overall well-being.

Beyond these specific techniques, simply incorporating more sound into your daily routine can be beneficial for managing anxiety. Listening to calming music while commuting, working, or relaxing can help to create a more peaceful and centered state of mind. Taking a few minutes each day to engage in a mindful listening practice, where you focus your attention on the sounds around you without judgment, can also be helpful for cultivating awareness and reducing stress.

The key to using sound for anxiety relief is to find what works best for you. Experiment with different types of sounds, tempos, and rhythms to discover what resonates with you most deeply. Create playlists of calming music, nature sounds, or binaural beats that you can listen to whenever you feel anxious or overwhelmed. Consider attending a sound bath or sound healing session to experience the immersive and transformative power of sound.

Sound is a powerful tool that can be used to quiet the anxious mind, promote relaxation, and restore inner peace. By incorporating sound into your daily routine and exploring the various sonic modalities available, you can create a personalized sound therapy practice that supports your mental and emotional well-being. Remember, finding your sonic solutions for anxiety is a journey of self-discovery, so be patient, experiment, and trust your intuition to guide you towards the sounds that soothe your soul and calm your mind.

ᗡᗡᗡ

*The stories of those who have found healing through sound are a testament to its transformative power. Let their experiences inspire you to embark on your own sonic adventure and discover the profound impact sound can have on your life.*

# THIRTEEN

# Sound Healing for Trauma: A Gentle Path to Emotional Healing

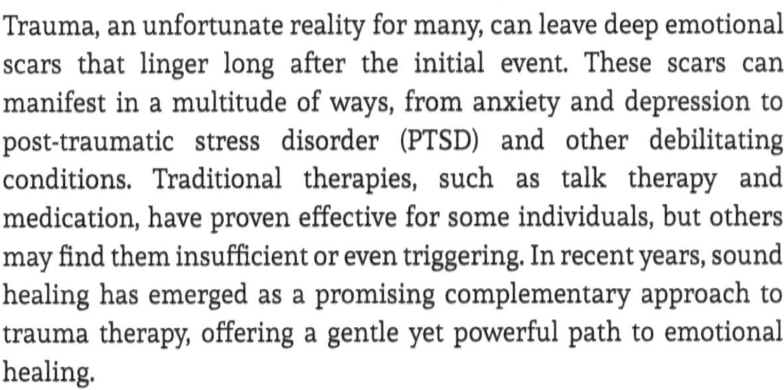

Trauma, an unfortunate reality for many, can leave deep emotional scars that linger long after the initial event. These scars can manifest in a multitude of ways, from anxiety and depression to post-traumatic stress disorder (PTSD) and other debilitating conditions. Traditional therapies, such as talk therapy and medication, have proven effective for some individuals, but others may find them insufficient or even triggering. In recent years, sound healing has emerged as a promising complementary approach to trauma therapy, offering a gentle yet powerful path to emotional healing.

The use of sound for healing is not a new concept. Ancient cultures around the world have long recognized the power of sound to soothe the soul, uplift the spirit, and promote physical and emotional well-being. From the rhythmic drumming of indigenous tribes to the chanting of Buddhist monks, sound has been used for centuries to facilitate healing and transformation.

Modern sound healing draws upon these ancient traditions, incorporating various techniques and modalities to address the complex needs of trauma survivors. One of the key principles underlying sound healing is the understanding that trauma is not just a psychological phenomenon, but also a physiological one. Trauma can disrupt the nervous system, leading to a state of hyperarousal or dissociation. This dysregulation can manifest in a variety of symptoms, such as anxiety, hypervigilance, flashbacks, nightmares, and difficulty regulating emotions.

Sound healing offers a unique way to address this dysregulation by working directly with the nervous system. Sound vibrations can bypass the conscious mind and access deeper levels of the subconscious, where traumatic memories and emotions are often stored. By creating a safe and supportive environment, sound healers can use specific frequencies and rhythms to help trauma survivors release pent-up emotions, regulate their nervous systems, and reconnect with their bodies.

One of the most common tools used in sound healing for trauma is the singing bowl. These ancient instruments, typically made of metal or crystal, produce rich, resonant tones that can have a deeply relaxing and grounding effect. The vibrations produced by the singing bowls can help to calm the nervous system, reduce anxiety, and promote a sense of peace and well-being.

Another powerful tool is the drum. The rhythmic beat of a drum can induce a trance-like state, allowing trauma survivors to access and process buried emotions. Drumming circles, which involve a group of people drumming together, can also create a sense of community and connection, which can be especially healing for those who have experienced isolation or disconnection as a result of trauma.

Sound healing is not limited to traditional instruments. Many practitioners also use tuning forks, gongs, chimes, and even their own voices to create healing soundscapes. These sounds can be used to entrain brainwave patterns, induce relaxation, and promote emotional release. Some sound healers also incorporate guided imagery, meditation, and breathwork into their sessions, creating a holistic approach to trauma healing.

The benefits of sound healing for trauma are numerous and varied. Many individuals report experiencing a reduction in anxiety, depression, and PTSD symptoms. Sound healing can also help to improve sleep, boost mood, and enhance overall well-being. Some individuals even report experiencing a sense of closure and resolution around past traumas.

One of the most important aspects of sound healing for trauma is that it is a gentle and non-invasive approach. Unlike traditional therapies, which can sometimes be confrontational or triggering, sound healing offers a safe and supportive space for individuals to explore their emotions and heal at their own pace. This is particularly important for trauma survivors, who may be sensitive to triggers and may need a more gentle approach to healing.

It is important to note that sound healing is not a substitute for traditional therapy. It is best used as a complementary approach, in conjunction with other forms of treatment. If you are considering sound healing for trauma, it is important to find a qualified practitioner who has experience working with trauma survivors.

Sound healing offers a gentle path to emotional healing for those who have experienced trauma. By working directly with the nervous system and creating a safe and supportive environment, sound healers can help individuals release pent-up emotions, regulate their nervous systems, and reconnect with their bodies. While sound healing is not a cure-all, it can be a powerful tool for promoting healing and transformation, offering a ray of hope to those who have suffered from the debilitating effects of trauma.

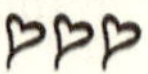

*A sound mind in a sound body is not just a proverb; it is a blueprint for holistic health. By nurturing both our physical and mental well-being, we create a symphony of balance and vitality that allows us to thrive.*

# FOURTEEN

# Sonic Tools for Focus & Productivity: Boosting Your Brainpower

In our modern age of relentless distractions, maintaining focus and achieving peak productivity can feel like an uphill battle. The constant barrage of notifications, emails, and social media updates can easily derail our concentration and leave us feeling overwhelmed and scattered. Fortunately, a powerful ally exists in an unexpected place: sound.

While often associated with entertainment and leisure, sound can be a potent tool for enhancing cognitive function, sharpening focus, and boosting productivity.

By strategically utilizing specific sounds and auditory techniques, we can create a sonic environment that optimizes our brainpower and empowers us to achieve our goals.

The relationship between sound and productivity is rooted in the intricate workings of our brains. Our brains are constantly bombarded with sensory information, and sound plays a crucial role in filtering and processing this information.

Certain types of sounds can help to filter out distractions, improve attention, and enhance cognitive performance.

One such type of sound is ambient noise. Ambient noise is a consistent, low-level background sound that can help to mask distracting noises and create a more focused environment. Studies have shown that listening to ambient noise, such as the sound of rain, white noise, or even the hum of a fan, can improve focus, concentration, and creativity.

Another powerful sonic tool for productivity is music. Music has a profound impact on our moods and emotions, and can be used to create a positive and motivating work environment.

Upbeat, rhythmic music can boost energy levels and motivation, while calming, instrumental music can help to reduce stress and anxiety. The key is to choose music that matches your personal preferences and the task at hand.

Binaural beats and isochronic tones, which are specific frequencies of sound that can entrain brainwave patterns, offer another promising avenue for enhancing focus and productivity. These sounds, when listened to through headphones, can induce a state of heightened alertness and concentration by synchronizing brainwave activity with the desired frequency.

Research suggests that binaural beats and isochronic tones may be particularly effective for improving focus, memory, and cognitive performance.

Nature sounds, such as the gentle rustling of leaves, the rhythmic crashing of waves, or the soothing chirping of birds, can also be incredibly effective for boosting brainpower.

These sounds are often rich in calming frequencies, such as alpha and theta brainwaves, which are associated with relaxation, creativity, and problem-solving. Spending time in nature or listening to recordings of nature sounds can help to clear the mind, reduce stress, and enhance cognitive function.

The use of sound for productivity is not limited to listening to specific sounds. The act of creating sound can also be beneficial for focus and concentration.

Playing a musical instrument, singing, or even humming can help to engage the brain and promote a state of flow, where we are fully immersed in the task at hand and time seems to melt away. This state of flow is often associated with peak performance and creativity.

Incorporating sonic tools for focus and productivity into your daily routine can be as simple as listening to a playlist of ambient noise or nature sounds while you work. You can also experiment with binaural beats or isochronic tones, or try playing a musical instrument or singing during your breaks.

If you have the opportunity, spending time in nature can also be a powerful way to boost your brainpower and enhance your overall well-being.

The key is to find what works best for you. Everyone responds to sound differently, so it's important to experiment with different types of sounds and auditory techniques to discover what helps you to focus and be most productive.

Once you find what works, make it a regular part of your routine and reap the benefits of a more focused, productive, and creative mind.

Sound is a powerful tool that can be used to unlock our full potential. By harnessing the power of sound, we can create a sonic environment that supports our cognitive function, enhances our focus, and boosts our productivity.

In a world that is constantly demanding our attention, sound can be a much-needed ally in our quest for peak performance and well-being.

ppp

*Your life is a symphony of sounds, waiting to be composed. Choose the notes that resonate with your soul, and let them guide you towards a life filled with peace, harmony, and joy.*

# FIFTEEN

# SOUND & MOVEMENT: COMBINING SOUND & GENTLE MOVEMENT FOR STRESS RELIEF

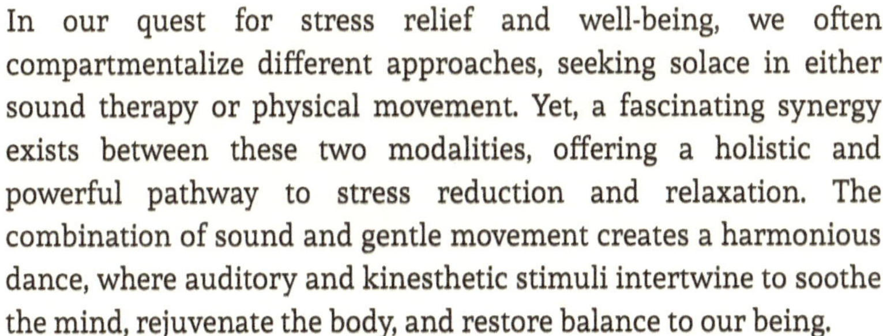

In our quest for stress relief and well-being, we often compartmentalize different approaches, seeking solace in either sound therapy or physical movement. Yet, a fascinating synergy exists between these two modalities, offering a holistic and powerful pathway to stress reduction and relaxation. The combination of sound and gentle movement creates a harmonious dance, where auditory and kinesthetic stimuli intertwine to soothe the mind, rejuvenate the body, and restore balance to our being.

The human experience is inherently multisensory, with our various senses working in concert to create a rich and vibrant tapestry of perception. Sound and movement, in particular, share a deep connection, as both are forms of vibration that resonate with our bodies on a cellular level. When we move to music, our bodies naturally synchronize with the rhythm, creating a sense of flow and harmony. This synchronization is not just a physical phenomenon; it also extends to our mental and emotional states, fostering a sense of calmness, joy, and well-being.

The practice of combining sound and movement for stress relief has roots in ancient traditions. Indigenous cultures around the world have long used dance, music, and ritualistic movement as a means of healing, celebration, and spiritual connection. These practices recognized the interconnectedness of mind, body, and spirit, and sought to create harmony and balance through the integration of sound and movement.

Modern science is now catching up with this ancient wisdom, uncovering the neurological and physiological mechanisms that underlie the therapeutic effects of sound and movement. Research has shown that both sound and movement can stimulate the release of endorphins, the body's natural painkillers and mood elevators. They can also activate the parasympathetic nervous system, responsible for rest and relaxation, counteracting the effects of stress and promoting a state of calm.

Moreover, sound and movement can have a profound impact on our brainwaves, the electrical patterns that reflect our mental state. Different brainwave frequencies are associated with different states of consciousness, from deep sleep (delta waves) to focused attention (beta waves). Certain types of sound and movement, such as slow, rhythmic music and gentle swaying, can induce a state of deep relaxation and calmness, characterized by alpha and theta brainwaves. This state is conducive to stress reduction, emotional healing, and creative expression.

The specific type of movement used in conjunction with sound can vary depending on individual preferences and needs. Some people may find that gentle stretching or yoga poses, accompanied by calming music or nature sounds, create a sense of grounding and relaxation. Others may prefer more dynamic movement, such as dancing or tai chi, set to upbeat or rhythmic music. The key is to find a combination of sound and movement that feels enjoyable and promotes a sense of flow and connection to the body.

The benefits of combining sound and movement for stress relief are numerous and varied. Physically, it can help to reduce muscle tension, improve flexibility, and enhance coordination. Emotionally, it can help to release pent-up emotions, reduce anxiety, and promote feelings of joy and well-being. Mentally, it can help to clear the mind, improve focus, and enhance creativity.

This approach is particularly effective for individuals who struggle with traditional forms of stress relief, such as meditation or talk therapy. The combination of sound and movement provides a multisensory experience that can be more engaging and accessible than purely cognitive or verbal approaches. It also allows for a deeper level of emotional expression and release, as movement can often facilitate the expression of emotions that are difficult to put into words.

Incorporating sound and movement into your daily routine can be as simple as putting on some music and dancing around your living room, or taking a yoga class set to calming music. You can also explore more specialized practices, such as sound healing dance or movement meditation. The key is to find a practice that resonates with you and that you can commit to on a regular basis.

The combination of sound and movement is a powerful and versatile tool for stress relief and well-being. By harnessing the synergistic effects of these two modalities, we can create a harmonious dance that nourishes our bodies, minds, and spirits. Whether you are a seasoned dancer or a novice mover, the power of sound and movement is available to all who seek it. So let the music move you, and let the movement set your spirit free.

ᴘᴘᴘ

*Sound is a gift, a universal language that speaks to the depths of our being. Embrace its power to heal, inspire, and transform, and let it be your guide on a journey towards a more fulfilling and joyful life.*

# SIXTEEN

# SOUND & MINDFULNESS: TUNING INTO THE PRESENT MOMENT

In the whirlwind of modern life, our minds are often caught in a ceaseless stream of thoughts, worries, and distractions. The past haunts us with regrets, the future beckons with anxieties, and the present moment, the only reality we truly have, slips through our fingers like sand. Mindfulness, the practice of paying non-judgmental attention to the present moment, offers a powerful antidote to this mental chaos. And sound, with its ability to anchor us in the here and now, can be a profound ally in our journey towards mindfulness.

At its core, mindfulness is about cultivating awareness of our present-moment experience, including our thoughts, emotions, bodily sensations, and the world around us. It is about observing these experiences without judgment or reactivity, allowing them to come and go like waves on a beach. By cultivating mindfulness, we can break free from the grip of habitual patterns of thinking and reacting, and develop a deeper sense of inner peace and well-being.

Sound plays a pivotal role in our experience of the present moment. It is a constant stream of information that bombards our senses, providing us with clues about our environment and our internal state. By tuning into the sounds around us, we can anchor ourselves in the present moment and cultivate a deeper sense of awareness.

One of the simplest ways to incorporate sound into mindfulness practice is through mindful listening. This involves intentionally focusing our attention on the sounds that are present in our environment, without judgment or evaluation. We can listen to the sounds of nature, such as the rustling of leaves, the chirping of birds, or the gentle lapping of waves. We can also listen to the sounds of our own bodies, such as our breath, our heartbeat, or the subtle sensations of movement.

As we listen, we simply observe the sounds as they arise and fall away, without getting caught up in thoughts or stories about them. We notice the qualities of each sound, such as its pitch, volume, and timbre. We may notice how the sounds change over time, or how they interact with each other. By paying close attention to the details of our auditory experience, we can cultivate a deeper sense of presence and awareness.

Another way to use sound for mindfulness is through sound meditation. This involves listening to specific sounds, such as chanting, singing bowls, or nature recordings, with the intention of focusing the mind and cultivating a state of inner peace. Sound meditation can help to quiet the mental chatter, reduce stress and anxiety, and promote deep relaxation.

The rhythmic nature of sound can also be used to anchor us in the present moment. By focusing on the rhythm of our breath or the beat of a drum, we can cultivate a sense of grounding and stability.

Rhythmic sounds can also induce a state of trance or meditation, where the mind becomes more receptive to inner wisdom and insight.

Sound can also be used to create a sense of spaciousness and expansiveness, which can be helpful for individuals who feel trapped or constricted by their thoughts and emotions. Listening to sounds that evoke a sense of vastness, such as the sound of the ocean or the wind in the trees, can help to open up our awareness and create a feeling of interconnectedness with the world around us.

Incorporating sound into mindfulness practice can be a powerful way to deepen our awareness, cultivate inner peace, and connect with the present moment. Whether through mindful listening, sound meditation, or simply paying attention to the sounds of our daily lives, sound can be a valuable tool for enhancing our mindfulness practice and enriching our lives.

As we continue to explore the intersection of sound and mindfulness, we are discovering new and innovative ways to harness the power of sound for healing and transformation. From sound therapy to sound baths to sonic meditation apps, the possibilities are endless. By embracing the power of sound, we can tune into the present moment, cultivate greater awareness, and live more fully in each and every breath.

ৡৡৡ

*Stress, a silent thief of joy, can be vanquished by the gentle touch of sound. Let the soothing melodies of nature, the rhythmic beats of music, or the resonant tones of a singing bowl wash over you, dissolving tension and restoring inner peace.*

# SEVENTEEN

## SOUND & BREATHWORK: DEEPENING RELAXATION WITH SOUND & BREATH

In the pursuit of relaxation and inner peace, the ancient practices of sound therapy and breathwork have emerged as powerful allies. Individually, each modality offers unique benefits for calming the mind, reducing stress, and promoting overall well-being. However, when combined, their synergistic effects create a profound experience of deep relaxation and healing. The harmonious interplay of sound and breath can unlock hidden depths of tranquility, enhance self-awareness, and facilitate a profound connection between mind, body, and spirit.

Breath, the essence of life, is a rhythmic dance that sustains our existence. It is an automatic function, yet it is also a tool that we can consciously harness to influence our physical and emotional states. Conscious breathing, also known as pranayama in yoga traditions, involves deliberately controlling the breath's pace, depth, and rhythm. This practice has been shown to have a wide range of benefits, including reducing stress, lowering blood pressure, improving sleep, and boosting mood.

Sound, on the other hand, is a vibration that travels through the air and interacts with our bodies on a cellular level. Different sounds have different frequencies and qualities, and these can affect our physiology and emotions in various ways. Certain sounds, such as the gentle hum of a Tibetan singing bowl or the rhythmic beat of a drum, can induce a state of deep relaxation and calmness.

When sound and breathwork are combined, a powerful synergy emerges. The rhythmic nature of sound can help to regulate the breath, creating a sense of ease and flow. The vibrations of sound can also help to release tension and blockages in the body, allowing the breath to flow more freely. In turn, the conscious control of the breath can help to deepen our awareness of the sound, enhancing its therapeutic effects.

One of the most common ways to combine sound and breathwork is through guided meditation. In these practices, a facilitator will lead participants through a series of breathing exercises while playing calming music or nature sounds. The combination of sound and guided breathwork can help to quiet the mind, reduce anxiety, and promote deep relaxation.

Another popular approach is sound baths, where participants lie down or sit comfortably while a practitioner plays a variety of instruments, such as singing bowls, gongs, chimes, and drums. The vibrations produced by these instruments wash over the body, creating a deeply relaxing and meditative state. Breathwork can be incorporated into sound baths by encouraging participants to synchronize their breath with the rhythm of the sounds, further enhancing the relaxation response.

The benefits of combining sound and breathwork for relaxation are numerous and varied. Physically, it can help to reduce muscle tension, lower blood pressure, and improve circulation. Emotionally, it can help to reduce anxiety, depression, and stress. Mentally, it can help to improve focus, clarity, and creativity. Spiritually, it can help to promote a sense of connection to oneself and the universe.

This approach is particularly effective for individuals who struggle with traditional relaxation techniques, such as meditation or yoga. The combination of sound and breathwork provides a multisensory experience that can be more engaging and accessible. It also allows for a deeper level of relaxation, as the sound and breathwork synergistically reinforce each other's effects.

Incorporating sound and breathwork into your daily routine can be as simple as listening to calming music while practicing deep breathing exercises. You can also explore more specialized practices, such as guided meditations or sound baths. The key is to find a practice that resonates with you and that you can commit to on a regular basis.

As with any form of therapy or self-care practice, it is important to consult with a qualified practitioner if you have any underlying health conditions or concerns. While sound and breathwork are generally considered safe and effective, they may not be suitable for everyone.

The combination of sound and breathwork offers a profound and accessible pathway to deep relaxation and healing. By harnessing the power of these two ancient modalities, we can tap into our innate capacity for self-regulation, reduce stress, and cultivate a greater sense of well-being. Whether you are seeking relief from anxiety, insomnia, or chronic pain, or simply looking to deepen your relaxation practice, the harmonious interplay of sound and breath can guide you on a journey of profound transformation.

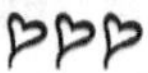

*The anxious mind, a whirlwind of thoughts and worries, can find solace in the gentle embrace of sound. Let calming music, binaural beats, or nature sounds create a sanctuary of tranquility where your mind can rest and find peace.*

# EIGHTEEN

# Sonic Spaces: Creating a Peaceful Home Environment with Sound

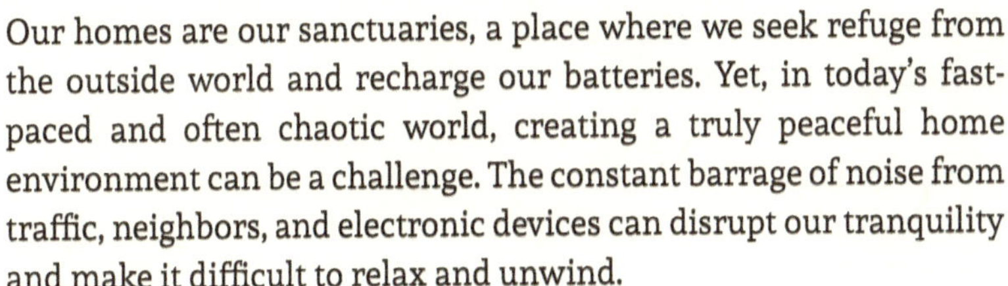

Our homes are our sanctuaries, a place where we seek refuge from the outside world and recharge our batteries. Yet, in today's fast-paced and often chaotic world, creating a truly peaceful home environment can be a challenge. The constant barrage of noise from traffic, neighbors, and electronic devices can disrupt our tranquility and make it difficult to relax and unwind.

Fortunately, we can harness the power of sound to transform our homes into havens of peace and serenity. By thoughtfully curating our sonic environment, we can create a space that nurtures our well-being, promotes relaxation, and enhances our overall quality of life.

The concept of sonic spaces is rooted in the understanding that sound has a profound impact on our moods, emotions, and even our physiology. Different sounds evoke different responses in us, from feelings of joy and excitement to anxiety and stress.

By carefully selecting and arranging sounds in our homes, we can create a sonic landscape that supports our desired emotional and mental states.

One of the first steps in creating a peaceful sonic space is to minimize unwanted noise. This can be achieved through a variety of methods, such as soundproofing walls and windows, using noise-canceling headphones, or simply closing doors and windows to block out external sounds.

Investing in soft furnishings, such as rugs, curtains, and upholstered furniture, can also help to absorb sound and create a quieter environment.

Once unwanted noise has been minimized, we can begin to introduce sounds that promote relaxation and well-being. Nature sounds, such as the gentle rustling of leaves, the rhythmic crashing of waves, or the soothing chirping of birds, have been shown to have a calming effect on the nervous system.

These sounds can be played through speakers, sound machines, or even smartphone apps, creating a virtual oasis of tranquility in your home.

Music can also be a powerful tool for creating a peaceful sonic environment. Slow, melodic music with a tempo of around 60 beats per minute has been found to be particularly effective for inducing relaxation and reducing stress.

Consider creating playlists of calming music that you can play throughout the day, or choose a specific genre, such as classical or ambient music, that you find particularly soothing.

Another way to enhance the sonic environment of your home is to incorporate natural sound elements. This can include things like water features, wind chimes, or even a small indoor fountain. The gentle sound of flowing water can be incredibly relaxing, while the melodic tones of wind chimes can add a touch of whimsy and charm to your space.

In addition to these natural sound elements, you can also introduce sound-absorbing materials into your home décor. This can include things like acoustic panels, wall hangings, or even plants. These materials can help to reduce echoes and reverberations, creating a more acoustically pleasing environment.

The placement of sound sources is also an important consideration. Strategically placing speakers or sound machines throughout your home can help to create a more immersive and balanced sonic experience. For example, you may want to place a sound machine in your bedroom to help you fall asleep, or a speaker in your living room to create a relaxing atmosphere for entertaining guests.

When creating a peaceful sonic space, it's important to consider the individual preferences of everyone who lives in the home. What one person finds relaxing, another may find irritating. It's important to communicate with your family or roommates about their sonic preferences and to create a space that feels welcoming and comfortable for everyone.

Creating a peaceful home environment with sound is an ongoing process. As your needs and preferences change, so too should your sonic space. Don't be afraid to experiment with different sounds, textures, and placements until you find what works best for you.

By paying attention to the sounds in your home and making conscious choices about how you use sound, you can create a space that nurtures your well-being and supports your overall quality of life.

The benefits of a peaceful sonic environment are numerous and varied. It can reduce stress and anxiety, improve sleep, boost mood, enhance creativity, and promote relaxation. It can also create a more welcoming and inviting atmosphere for you and your guests. By investing in your sonic environment, you are investing in your own well-being and happiness.

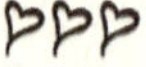

*Trauma, a deep wound that lingers, can be soothed by the gentle vibrations of sound. Allow the healing tones of singing bowls, gongs, or drums to wash over you, releasing emotional blockages and facilitating a journey of recovery and renewal.*

# NINETEEN

## Sonic Technology: Exploring Apps & Devices for Stress Relief

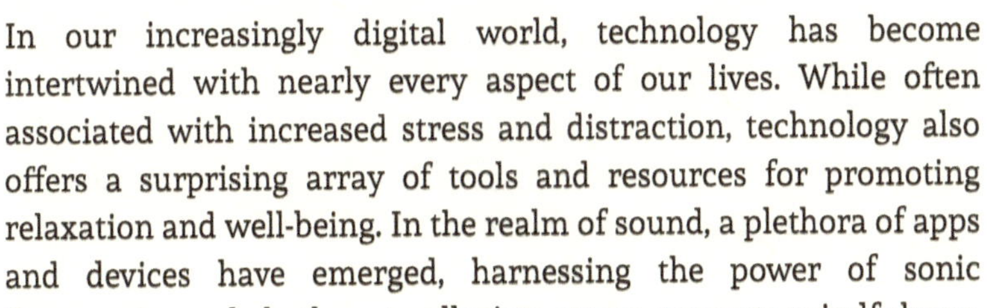

In our increasingly digital world, technology has become intertwined with nearly every aspect of our lives. While often associated with increased stress and distraction, technology also offers a surprising array of tools and resources for promoting relaxation and well-being. In the realm of sound, a plethora of apps and devices have emerged, harnessing the power of sonic frequencies and rhythms to alleviate stress, promote mindfulness, and enhance overall mental health.

The convergence of sound therapy and technology has opened up new avenues for accessing and utilizing the therapeutic benefits of sound. No longer confined to traditional instruments or live performances, sound healing is now readily available at our fingertips, accessible through a wide range of digital platforms and devices. This accessibility has democratized the practice of sound therapy, allowing individuals to incorporate it into their daily lives with ease and convenience.

One of the most popular ways to explore sonic technology for stress relief is through mobile apps. These apps offer a vast library of sounds, music, and guided meditations designed to promote relaxation, reduce anxiety, and improve sleep. Many of these apps also incorporate features such as binaural beats and isochronic tones, which are specific frequencies of sound that can entrain brainwave patterns and induce different states of consciousness.

Binaural beats, for example, are created by playing two slightly different frequencies of sound, one to each ear. The brain perceives the difference between these two frequencies as a third, phantom beat, known as the binaural beat. This beat, which is not actually present in the external sound, is believed to induce a state of brainwave entrainment, where the brain's electrical activity begins to synchronize with the frequency of the binaural beat.

Isochronic tones, on the other hand, are single tones that are pulsed on and off at regular intervals, creating a rhythmic beat. Like binaural beats, isochronic tones can also induce brainwave entrainment, leading to changes in mental and physical states. Both binaural beats and isochronic tones have been studied for their potential to improve sleep, reduce anxiety, and enhance relaxation.

In addition to binaural beats and isochronic tones, many sound therapy apps also offer guided meditations that incorporate various relaxation techniques, such as deep breathing exercises, progressive muscle relaxation, and visualization. These guided meditations can help to quiet the mind, reduce stress, and promote a sense of inner peace.

Another popular sonic technology for stress relief is the use of white noise machines. White noise is a consistent sound that covers a wide range of frequencies, similar to the static on a radio. It can be used to mask distracting noises and create a more peaceful sleep environment. White noise machines are often used by individuals who struggle with insomnia or who live in noisy environments.

For those seeking a more immersive sound experience, sound machines that offer nature sounds, such as the sound of rain, ocean waves, or a crackling fire, can be particularly effective for promoting relaxation and stress relief. These sounds can evoke a sense of tranquility and connection to nature, even in the midst of a bustling city.

Beyond apps and sound machines, wearable technology is also emerging as a promising tool for sound-based stress relief. Some wearable devices, such as smartwatches and fitness trackers, now offer guided meditations and relaxation exercises that incorporate sound. These devices can also track heart rate, sleep patterns, and other physiological data, providing valuable insights into how sound affects our bodies and minds.

As technology continues to evolve, the possibilities for sonic solutions for stress relief are only expanding. Virtual reality (VR) and augmented reality (AR) technologies are being explored as a way to create immersive sound environments that can transport users to tranquil settings, such as a peaceful forest or a secluded beach. These technologies have the potential to provide a powerful escape from the stresses of daily life and offer a unique form of sound therapy.

While sonic technology offers a wealth of resources for stress relief, it's important to remember that it is not a substitute for professional help. If you are struggling with chronic or severe anxiety, it's important to seek guidance from a qualified healthcare provider.

However, for those seeking a complementary approach to stress management, sonic technology can be a valuable tool.

Incorporating sonic technology into your daily routine can be as simple as downloading a sound therapy app or listening to calming music while you work. You can also experiment with different devices and techniques to find what works best for you. The key is to make sound a conscious part of your life and to use it as a tool to promote relaxation, well-being, and inner peace.

♭♭♭

*Focus, a fleeting companion in a world of distractions, can be summoned by the power of sound. Let ambient noise, binaural beats, or the rhythmic pulse of music sharpen your concentration and unlock your full potential.*

# TWENTY

## SOUND & COMMUNITY: THE POWER OF SHARED SONIC EXPERIENCES

Throughout human history, sound has served as a unifying force, weaving a rich tapestry of shared experiences that transcend cultural boundaries and individual differences. From the rhythmic chants of ancient rituals to the electrifying energy of a live concert, the power of sound to connect us on a deep emotional and spiritual level is undeniable.

The shared sonic experiences we encounter in our communities, whether through music, spoken word, or the natural soundscapes that surround us, have a profound impact on our sense of belonging, identity, and well-being.

The human voice, arguably the most primal and expressive instrument, has long been a conduit for shared sonic experiences. From lullabies sung to infants to the powerful oratory of political leaders, the human voice carries a unique power to convey emotions, inspire action, and forge connections between individuals and groups.

Throughout history, communities have gathered to share stories, sing songs, and recite prayers, creating a sense of shared identity and purpose through the power of the spoken and sung word.

Music, in its many forms, is perhaps the most universal language of sound. Whether it's the infectious rhythms of a drum circle, the soaring melodies of a symphony orchestra, or the heartfelt lyrics of a folk song, music has an uncanny ability to transcend cultural barriers and touch the depths of our souls.

Shared musical experiences, such as concerts, festivals, and jam sessions, create a sense of collective energy and euphoria, fostering a sense of belonging and connection that can be transformative.

Beyond music, there are countless other ways in which sound can bring communities together. The sounds of nature, such as the rustling of leaves, the crashing of waves, or the chirping of birds, can evoke a sense of awe and wonder, reminding us of our interconnectedness with the natural world.

Shared experiences in nature, such as hiking, camping, or simply sitting in a park, can be deeply enriching and restorative, allowing us to connect with each other and the world around us in a meaningful way.

Religious and spiritual practices often incorporate sound as a central element. The chanting of mantras, the ringing of bells, and the singing of hymns create a sacred sonic space that fosters a sense of reverence, devotion, and community. These shared sonic experiences can transcend individual differences and create a feeling of unity and shared purpose among those who participate.

Sound also plays a crucial role in cultural traditions and celebrations. From the vibrant drumming of African festivals to the raucous cheers of a sporting event, sound can create a sense of excitement, anticipation, and shared identity. These shared sonic experiences can strengthen cultural bonds, reinforce community values, and create lasting memories.

In recent years, technology has expanded the possibilities for shared sonic experiences. Online platforms and social media have allowed us to connect with people from all over the world, sharing music, stories, and other sonic expressions in real-time.

Virtual concerts, online sound baths, and even social media challenges that involve creating and sharing sounds have become increasingly popular, offering new ways to connect with others through the power of sound.

The impact of shared sonic experiences on our well-being is profound. Studies have shown that singing in a choir, attending a concert, or even simply listening to music with others can reduce stress, boost mood, and enhance feelings of social connection. Shared sonic experiences can also strengthen social bonds, promote empathy and understanding, and foster a sense of belonging and community.

The power of sound to bring people together is evident in times of crisis and adversity. In the aftermath of natural disasters, terrorist attacks, or other traumatic events, communities often turn to music and other forms of sound to express their grief, offer solace, and rebuild their sense of connection. Shared sonic experiences can provide a sense of hope, resilience, and solidarity in the face of adversity.

In a world that is increasingly fragmented and polarized, the power of shared sonic experiences is more important than ever. Sound can bridge cultural divides, transcend language barriers, and create a sense of unity and belonging.

Whether it's through music, nature sounds, religious practices, or cultural traditions, the shared sonic experiences we encounter in our communities have the power to heal, inspire, and connect us on a deep and meaningful level. Let us embrace the power of sound and celebrate the rich tapestry of shared sonic experiences that make us human.

ᐅᐅᐅ

*The sounds of nature, a symphony of whispers and rhythms, have the power to transport us to a place of tranquility and peace. Immerse yourself in their soothing embrace, and let their gentle melodies wash away your worries and restore your connection to the natural world.*

# TWENTY-ONE

# THE FUTURE OF SOUND HEALING: EMERGING TRENDS & TECHNOLOGIES

Sound, an ancient and universal language, has long been recognized for its profound impact on human well-being. From the rhythmic chants of indigenous cultures to the harmonious melodies of classical music, sound has the power to soothe, heal, and inspire. In recent years, the field of sound healing has experienced a renaissance, fueled by advancements in technology and a growing body of scientific evidence supporting its efficacy. As we look to the future, the landscape of sound healing is evolving rapidly, with emerging trends and technologies poised to revolutionize the way we approach health and wellness.

One of the most exciting developments in sound healing is the integration of virtual reality (VR) and augmented reality (AR) technologies. These immersive technologies have the potential to transport users to virtual soundscapes, where they can experience the therapeutic benefits of sound in a multi-sensory environment. Imagine walking through a lush forest, surrounded by the sounds of chirping birds and rustling leaves, or meditating in a tranquil temple, bathed in the resonant tones of singing bowls and gongs. VR and AR can create a sense of presence and immersion that amplifies the effects of sound therapy, making it more accessible and engaging for individuals from all walks of life.

Another promising trend is the development of personalized sound therapy. With the advent of wearable technology and sophisticated algorithms, it is now possible to create customized sound experiences tailored to an individual's unique needs and preferences. By analyzing physiological data such as heart rate, brainwave patterns, and stress levels, personalized sound therapy can deliver targeted frequencies and rhythms that optimize relaxation, focus, and overall well-being. This approach has the potential to revolutionize the way we approach stress management, sleep disorders, and other health conditions.

Artificial intelligence (AI) is also playing an increasingly important role in the future of sound healing. AI-powered algorithms can analyze vast amounts of data to identify patterns and correlations between sound and physiological responses. This information can be used to develop more effective sound therapy protocols, as well as to create personalized sound experiences that are tailored to an individual's specific needs. AI can also be used to create interactive sound environments that respond to a user's emotional state, providing real-time feedback and support.

The field of bioacoustics, which explores the interaction between sound and living organisms, is also shedding new light on the mechanisms of sound healing. Research has shown that sound can influence cellular function, gene expression, and even the structure of DNA. This suggests that sound may have a more profound impact on our health than previously thought, with the potential to address not just symptoms but also the underlying causes of disease.

As our understanding of the science of sound deepens, we are also witnessing a growing interest in the use of sound for preventative health. Sound baths, sound meditations, and other sound-based practices are being incorporated into wellness programs and corporate settings, offering a proactive approach to stress reduction, mental health, and overall well-being. This trend is likely to continue as more and more individuals and organizations recognize the value of sound as a powerful tool for preventative health.

The future of sound healing is not just about technology, however. There is also a growing movement towards integrating sound therapy with other healing modalities, such as yoga, massage, and acupuncture. This holistic approach recognizes the interconnectedness of mind, body, and spirit, and seeks to address the root causes of dis-ease rather than just treating symptoms. By combining sound therapy with other practices, practitioners can create a more comprehensive and effective approach to healing.

Sound healing is also becoming more accessible and affordable, thanks to the proliferation of online resources and affordable sound therapy devices. This democratization of sound healing is making it possible for more people to experience its benefits, regardless of their socioeconomic status or geographic location.

In conclusion, the future of sound healing is bright and full of possibilities. With emerging technologies like VR, AR, and AI, personalized sound therapy, advancements in bioacoustics, and a growing emphasis on preventative health, the potential of sound to heal and transform is only just beginning to be realized. As we continue to explore the intricate relationship between sound and well-being, we can expect to see even more innovative and effective sound healing applications in the years to come. Whether through cutting-edge technology or ancient practices, sound will continue to play a vital role in our quest for health, happiness, and wholeness.

❥❥❥

*Sound is the universal language of the soul. It speaks to us in ways that words cannot, soothing our sorrows, igniting our passions, and awakening our spirits.*

# TWENTY-TWO

# EMPOWERING YOUR SONIC JOURNEY: TAKING CHARGE OF YOUR WELL-BEING

In the intricate tapestry of our lives, sound weaves an invisible thread that profoundly influences our well-being. From the rhythmic beating of our hearts to the harmonious melodies that uplift our spirits, sound is an ever-present force that shapes our emotions, thoughts, and physical states. By recognizing and harnessing the power of sound, we can embark on a transformative sonic journey, taking charge of our well-being and cultivating a life filled with harmony, balance, and joy.

Embarking on this sonic journey begins with developing a deeper understanding of how sound affects us. Sound is more than just a sensory experience; it is a vibration that resonates with every cell in our bodies. Different frequencies and rhythms of sound can elicit different responses in our nervous systems, influencing our emotions, thoughts, and physiological states. By becoming attuned to these subtle nuances, we can begin to make conscious choices about the sounds we expose ourselves to, creating a sonic environment that supports our well-being.

One of the first steps in empowering your sonic journey is to cultivate mindfulness around sound. This involves paying attention to the sounds that surround us in our daily lives, both the pleasant and the unpleasant. Notice how different sounds affect your mood, energy levels, and focus. Are there certain sounds that consistently leave you feeling agitated or stressed? Are there others that bring you a sense of calm and tranquility? By becoming aware of our sonic preferences and sensitivities, we can begin to make choices that support our well-being.

Once we have developed a greater awareness of sound, we can begin to explore the vast array of sonic tools and techniques available to us. Music, perhaps the most ubiquitous form of sound, has long been recognized for its therapeutic potential. Different genres and styles of music can evoke different emotions and physiological responses. Slow, melodic music can promote relaxation and reduce stress, while upbeat, rhythmic music can boost energy and motivation. Experiment with different types of music to discover what works best for you in different situations and moods.

Nature sounds, such as the gentle rustling of leaves, the rhythmic crashing of waves, or the soothing chirping of birds, can also be incredibly therapeutic. These sounds have a unique ability to calm the nervous system, reduce stress hormones, and promote relaxation. Spending time in nature or listening to recordings of nature sounds can be a powerful way to reconnect with the earth and find inner peace.

For those seeking a more immersive sonic experience, sound baths offer a unique way to bathe in the healing vibrations of sound. During a sound bath, participants lie down or sit comfortably in a quiet space while a practitioner plays a variety of instruments, such as singing bowls, gongs, chimes, and drums. The resonant tones and vibrations produced by these instruments wash over the body, creating a deeply relaxing and meditative state. Sound baths have been shown to reduce stress, anxiety, and pain, as well as improve sleep and overall well-being.

Binaural beats and isochronic tones, which are specific frequencies of sound that can entrain brainwave patterns, offer another promising avenue for enhancing well-being. These sounds, when listened to through headphones, can induce different states of consciousness, such as deep relaxation, focus, or creativity. While research on binaural beats and isochronic tones is still ongoing, preliminary studies suggest that they may be effective for a variety of purposes, including stress reduction, sleep improvement, and pain management.

Incorporating sonic practices into your daily routine can be a simple yet powerful way to enhance your well-being. Start your day with a few minutes of mindful listening, paying attention to the sounds around you. Create a playlist of calming music or nature sounds that you can listen to while commuting, working, or relaxing. Consider trying a sound bath or sound meditation session. Experiment with different sounds and techniques to discover what works best for you.

Empowering your sonic journey is not just about utilizing external sounds; it is also about tuning in to the sounds within. Our bodies are a symphony of vibrations, with each cell, organ, and system resonating at its own unique frequency. By cultivating awareness of our internal sounds, such as our breath, heartbeat, and even the subtle vibrations of our thoughts and emotions, we can gain valuable insights into our physical and emotional states.

This inner awareness can guide us in making choices that support our well-being. For example, if we notice that our breath is shallow and rapid, we can consciously slow it down and deepen it, activating the parasympathetic nervous system and promoting relaxation. If we notice that our thoughts are racing, we can use sound to anchor ourselves in the present moment and cultivate a sense of calm.

Empowering your sonic journey is an ongoing process of self-discovery and exploration. It is about reclaiming our innate connection to sound and using it as a tool for healing, growth, and transformation. By tuning into the symphony of sounds that surround us and within us, we can create a life that is rich in harmony, balance, and joy.

ᚦᚦᚦ

*In the tapestry of life, sound is the thread that weaves together our experiences, emotions, and memories. It is the soundtrack to our joys and sorrows, our triumphs and failures.*

# TWENTY-THREE

## SONIC SERENITY STORIES: INSPIRING TALES OF TRANSFORMATION

Sound, in its infinite variations and manifestations, has the profound ability to touch the human soul, to heal wounds both physical and emotional, and to inspire transformation. The stories of those who have embarked on sonic journeys are as diverse and unique as the individuals themselves, yet they all share a common thread: the power of sound to unlock a deeper sense of well-being, peace, and purpose.

Consider the story of Emily, a woman who had long struggled with anxiety and insomnia. Despite trying various therapies and medications, she continued to feel trapped in a cycle of worry and sleeplessness. It wasn't until she discovered the world of sound healing that her life began to change. Through a combination of sound baths, binaural beats, and nature sound therapy, Emily found herself able to quiet her mind, release tension, and finally experience the restful sleep she had longed for. As her anxiety diminished, she rediscovered her passion for life, her relationships blossomed, and she found a newfound sense of inner peace.

Then there's John, a veteran who had been diagnosed with PTSD after returning from combat. The trauma he had experienced left him with nightmares, flashbacks, and a constant sense of hypervigilance. Traditional therapies offered some relief, but it wasn't until he participated in a drumming circle for veterans that he truly began to heal. The rhythmic beat of the drums, combined with the camaraderie of fellow veterans, created a safe space for him to express his emotions, process his trauma, and reconnect with his sense of self. Over time, John's nightmares subsided, his flashbacks became less frequent, and he was able to reclaim his life.

For Sarah, a busy executive who struggled to find balance in her hectic life, sound became a lifeline. She had always loved music, but she never considered its potential for stress relief until she stumbled upon a sound meditation class. The guided meditation, accompanied by the soothing tones of Tibetan singing bowls, allowed Sarah to disconnect from the demands of her job and reconnect with her inner calm. As she incorporated sound meditation into her daily routine, she noticed a significant reduction in her stress levels, improved focus and concentration, and a newfound sense of clarity and purpose.

These are just a few examples of the countless stories of transformation that have emerged from the world of sound healing. Whether it's through music, nature sounds, sound baths, or other sonic modalities, people from all walks of life are discovering the power of sound to heal, inspire, and transform. These stories are a testament to the versatility and accessibility of sound healing, as well as its potential to address a wide range of physical, emotional, and spiritual challenges.

The beauty of sound healing lies in its ability to meet individuals where they are, offering a personalized and adaptable approach to well-being. Whether you're seeking relief from stress, anxiety, or chronic pain, or simply looking to enhance your creativity, focus, or sleep, there is a sonic solution out there for you. By exploring the vast landscape of sound, we can each discover the unique frequencies and rhythms that resonate with our own individual needs and preferences.

The stories of sonic transformation are not just inspiring; they are also empowering. They remind us that we have the power within ourselves to heal and create positive change in our lives. By embracing the power of sound, we can tap into our innate wisdom, creativity, and resilience. We can discover new ways of being, new perspectives on life, and new possibilities for growth and transformation.

Whether you're a seasoned sound healer or a curious newcomer, the stories of sonic transformation offer a glimpse into the infinite possibilities that sound holds for our well-being. They invite us to embark on our own sonic journeys, to explore the vast and ever-evolving landscape of sound, and to discover the unique frequencies that resonate with our souls. By opening ourselves to the transformative power of sound, we can create a life filled with harmony, balance, and joy.

ﻬﻬﻬ

*Sound is a bridge between the seen and the unseen, a portal to a world of infinite possibilities. It can transport us to distant lands, evoke long-forgotten memories, and connect us to the deeper mysteries of life.*

# TWENTY-FOUR

# A Sound Mind in a Sound Body: Cultivating Holistic Health

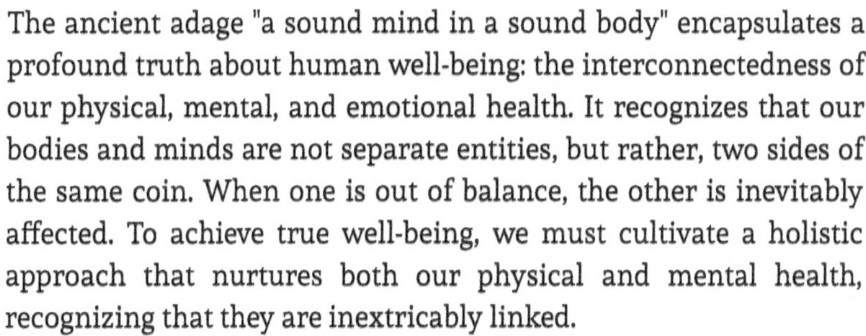

The ancient adage "a sound mind in a sound body" encapsulates a profound truth about human well-being: the interconnectedness of our physical, mental, and emotional health. It recognizes that our bodies and minds are not separate entities, but rather, two sides of the same coin. When one is out of balance, the other is inevitably affected. To achieve true well-being, we must cultivate a holistic approach that nurtures both our physical and mental health, recognizing that they are inextricably linked.

In our modern, fast-paced world, it's easy to become disconnected from our bodies and neglect our mental health. We often prioritize work, technology, and external achievements over self-care and inner peace. This imbalance can lead to a host of physical and mental ailments, from chronic stress and anxiety to heart disease and obesity. The good news is that we have the power to reclaim our health and well-being by adopting a holistic approach that honors the interconnectedness of mind and body.

One of the most powerful tools for cultivating holistic health is the practice of mindfulness. Mindfulness involves paying non-judgmental attention to the present moment, including our thoughts, emotions, bodily sensations, and the world around us. By cultivating mindfulness, we can develop a deeper understanding of our inner workings, become more aware of the signals our bodies are sending us, and make choices that support our overall well-being.

Mindfulness practices, such as meditation, yoga, and tai chi, have been shown to have a wide range of benefits for both physical and mental health. These practices can reduce stress, lower blood pressure, improve sleep, and boost mood. They can also help to increase self-awareness, compassion, and resilience. By incorporating mindfulness into our daily lives, we can cultivate a more balanced and harmonious state of being.

Another key aspect of holistic health is physical activity. Regular exercise is essential for maintaining a healthy body, but it also has profound benefits for our mental health. Exercise releases endorphins, natural mood boosters that can help to reduce stress, anxiety, and depression. It can also improve sleep, boost energy levels, and enhance cognitive function. Finding a form of exercise that you enjoy and can stick with is crucial for long-term success.

Nutrition also plays a vital role in holistic health. The food we eat provides the building blocks for our bodies and minds, so it's important to choose foods that nourish and support our overall well-being. A balanced diet that includes plenty of fruits, vegetables, whole grains, and lean protein can help to reduce inflammation, improve mood, and boost energy levels. Avoiding processed foods, sugary drinks, and excessive caffeine can also be beneficial for both physical and mental health.

In addition to these foundational practices, there are many other ways to cultivate holistic health. Spending time in nature has been shown to reduce stress, improve mood, and boost creativity. Connecting with others through meaningful relationships can also have a profound impact on our well-being. Practicing gratitude and cultivating a positive outlook on life can also help to reduce stress and improve overall happiness.

It's important to remember that holistic health is not a destination, but a journey. It's an ongoing process of self-discovery and self-care. There will be ups and downs along the way, but by prioritizing our well-being and making conscious choices that support our health, we can create a life that is rich in meaning, purpose, and joy.

The ancient wisdom of "a sound mind in a sound body" is as relevant today as it was centuries ago. By cultivating a holistic approach to health, we can achieve a state of balance and harmony that allows us to thrive in all areas of our lives. Let us embrace this wisdom and embark on a journey of self-discovery, healing, and transformation.

ᢒᢒᢒ

*The power of sound is not just in its ability to soothe and heal, but also in its ability to inspire and motivate. Let the rhythms of your favorite music propel you forward, the affirmations of a guided meditation empower you, and the sounds of nature awaken your sense of wonder.*

# TWENTY-FIVE

## YOUR SONIC SYMPHONY: CRAFTING A LIFE FILLED WITH PEACE & HARMONY

Life, in its essence, is a symphony of sounds. From the gentle rustling of leaves to the rhythmic beat of our hearts, we are constantly surrounded by a rich tapestry of auditory experiences. These sounds shape our emotions, influence our behaviors, and even impact our physical health. By consciously crafting our own sonic symphony, we can cultivate a life filled with peace, harmony, and well-being.

Imagine your life as a musical composition, where each sound represents a different note or instrument. The key to creating a harmonious symphony lies in understanding the different elements of sound and how they interact with each other. Tempo, rhythm, melody, harmony, and dynamics all play a role in shaping the overall mood and feel of a piece of music. Similarly, the sounds we choose to surround ourselves with can profoundly affect our emotional and mental states.

The first step in crafting your sonic symphony is to become aware of the sounds that currently fill your life. Take a moment to listen to the soundscape around you. What do you hear? Are there sounds that bring you joy and peace, or are there sounds that trigger stress and anxiety? By becoming mindful of the sounds that we expose ourselves to, we can begin to make conscious choices about the sonic environment we create for ourselves.

Once you have a better understanding of your current sonic landscape, you can start to make intentional changes. Begin by eliminating or minimizing the sounds that detract from your well-being. This might involve reducing exposure to loud or jarring noises, such as traffic, construction, or electronic devices. It might also mean creating boundaries around the types of music or media you consume, opting for calming and uplifting sounds rather than those that are aggressive or anxiety-inducing.

As you clear away the discordant notes, you can begin to introduce sounds that resonate with your soul and promote a sense of peace and harmony. Nature sounds, such as the gentle rustling of leaves, the rhythmic crashing of waves, or the soothing chirping of birds, have been shown to have a calming effect on the nervous system and reduce stress hormones. Incorporate these sounds into your daily life by spending time in nature, listening to nature sound recordings, or even creating a small indoor water feature.

Music is another powerful tool for crafting your sonic symphony. Choose music that aligns with your desired emotional state. If you're feeling stressed or anxious, opt for slow, melodic music with a calming rhythm. If you need a boost of energy or motivation, choose upbeat and rhythmic music. Experiment with different genres and artists to find what resonates with you most deeply.

Don't limit yourself to music and nature sounds. Explore other sonic modalities, such as singing bowls, tuning forks, or even your own voice. Chanting, humming, or toning can create vibrations that resonate with your body and mind, promoting relaxation and well-being. Sound baths, which involve immersing yourself in the sounds of various instruments, can also be a deeply relaxing and transformative experience.

As you curate your sonic symphony, pay attention to the rhythm of your life. Just as a piece of music has a natural flow and tempo, so too does our daily existence. By syncing your activities with your body's natural rhythms, you can optimize your energy levels, productivity, and overall well-being. This might involve aligning your sleep schedule with your circadian rhythm, scheduling breaks throughout the day to rest and recharge, or engaging in activities that promote relaxation and creativity.

Crafting a life filled with peace and harmony is an ongoing process. It requires a willingness to experiment, to listen to your intuition, and to adapt your sonic symphony as your needs and preferences change. By making sound a conscious part of your life, you can create a harmonious environment that supports your physical, emotional, and spiritual well-being.

Remember, your sonic symphony is unique to you. There is no right or wrong way to create it. The most important thing is to choose sounds that bring you joy, peace, and a sense of connection to yourself and the world around you. By embracing the power of sound, you can transform your life into a beautiful and harmonious masterpiece.

♭♭♭

*Embrace the sonic symphony that surrounds you. Listen to the whispers of the wind, the laughter of children, the melodies of your favorite songs. Let sound be your guide on a journey of self-discovery, healing, and transformation.*

# TWENTY-SIX
## SUMMARY

The power of sound to heal, inspire, and transform is a profound and often overlooked aspect of human experience. From the gentle rustling of leaves to the rhythmic beat of a drum, sound vibrations have a remarkable capacity to influence our physical, emotional, and spiritual well-being. Throughout this exploration, we have delved into the intricate ways in which sound can be harnessed to promote relaxation, reduce stress, enhance focus, and cultivate a deeper connection to ourselves and the world around us.

We began by unveiling the hidden healer within sound, understanding how it can harmonize our internal rhythms and promote a state of balance and coherence. We explored the science behind sound healing, delving into how sound waves interact with our bodies on a cellular level, influencing our physiology, emotions, and even our brainwave patterns. We discovered that specific frequencies and rhythms can trigger the release of neurotransmitters, such as dopamine and serotonin, which are associated with pleasure, relaxation, and well-being.

Nature's soundtrack, a symphony of gentle whispers and rhythmic patterns, emerged as a powerful tool for calming the nervous system and promoting relaxation. From the soothing sounds of rain and ocean waves to the melodic chirping of birds, nature's soundscapes offer a sanctuary of peace and tranquility amidst the chaos of modern life. We learned how to harness the calming power of natural sounds through mindful listening, nature sound recordings, and spending time in natural environments.

Music, a universal language that transcends cultural boundaries, also emerged as a potent medicine for the soul. We explored how different genres and styles of music can evoke a wide range of emotions and physiological responses, from the uplifting energy of upbeat pop music to the calming serenity of classical compositions. By curating personalized playlists and engaging in mindful listening, we can utilize music as a tool to reduce stress, improve mood, and enhance overall well-being.

Beyond music and nature sounds, we ventured into the realm of therapeutic soundscapes, exploring practices such as sound baths and the use of binaural beats and isochronic tones. Sound baths, with their immersive and multi-sensory experience, have been shown to promote deep relaxation, reduce anxiety, and facilitate emotional release. Binaural beats and isochronic tones, on the other hand, can entrain brainwave patterns, inducing states of calmness, focus, or creativity.

We also delved into the importance of incorporating sound into our daily routines, creating sonic self-care rituals that nourish our bodies and minds. From mindful listening practices to the creation of peaceful sonic spaces in our homes, we explored various ways to integrate sound into our lives and reap its therapeutic benefits.

The transformative power of sound extends beyond individual experiences. Shared sonic experiences, such as concerts, drumming circles, and religious ceremonies, have the power to unite communities, foster social connection, and promote collective well-being. By participating in these shared experiences, we can tap into a sense of belonging, purpose, and joy that transcends individual differences.

As we look to the future, the landscape of sound healing is rapidly evolving. Emerging technologies, such as virtual reality and artificial intelligence, are expanding the possibilities for sound therapy, offering new ways to experience and utilize the healing power of sound. Personalized sound therapy, based on individual needs and preferences, is also becoming increasingly accessible, promising a more tailored and effective approach to well-being.

Empowering our sonic journey is ultimately about taking charge of our well-being by consciously choosing the sounds that nourish our bodies, minds, and spirits. It is about cultivating mindfulness around sound, exploring the diverse sonic landscape, and incorporating sound-based practices into our daily lives. By doing so, we can create a life filled with peace, harmony, and joy.

In the grand symphony of life, sound plays a vital role, weaving a tapestry of emotions, memories, and experiences. By tuning into the melodies that resonate with our souls, we can unlock a deeper level of well-being, discover our true potential, and live a life that is truly harmonious.

♭♭♭

# Citation And References

This book represents the culmination of extensive research and meticulous analysis, incorporating a diverse range of sources, including numerous books, scholarly studies, and personal experiences. Additionally, I have scoured various websites to gather relevant information and data essential for the compilation of this work. I have taken every precaution to ensure the accuracy of the information presented and have diligently cited all sources to acknowledge their contributions.

Despite these efforts, the possibility of inadvertent errors remains. I deeply value the insights of my readers and appreciate any feedback that can help identify and rectify such inaccuracies. I encourage you to bring any discrepancies to my attention.

Your feedback is not only welcome but crucial, as it will aid in correcting current editions and enhancing the content of future ones. I am committed to maintaining the highest standards of accuracy and reliability in my work and thank you for your support and understanding.

Additionally, I firmly uphold the principle of freedom of speech and expression as guaranteed under Article 19(1)(a) of the Constitution of India, and I respect the diverse viewpoints and expressions of all readers.

ppp

# Other Books Of The Author

1. Empowering Minds: A Journey into Women's Self-Discovery and Power
2. The Dynamics of Motivation: Catalyzing Thought into Action
3. Meditation and Mental Well Being: The Path to Inner Peace and Clarity
4. The Psychology of Child Education: Nurturing Future Generations
5. Ethical Enlightenment: A Modern Guide to Living with Integrity
6. Voices of Empowerment: Stories of Women Rising Against Odds
7. Social Psychology in Everyday Life: Understanding Human Connections
8. The Essence of Motivational Speaking: Inspiring Change in Others
9. Balancing Acts: Women, Work, and the Will to Lead
10. Guiding with Grace: Raising Children with Compassion and Awareness
11. The Power of Positive Aging: Embracing Life After Fifty
12. Building Resilient Communities: Social Work in Action
13. The Ethical Educator: Principles for Teaching and Learning
14. From Insight to Impact: Social Psychology for a Better World
15. The Ethics of Empathy: A Guide to Ethical Living
16. The Science of Empowering the Self: Navigating Life's Challenges with Psychological Wisdom
17. The Mindful Conscious Leader: Meditation Techniques for Modern Management
18. Pioneering Spirit: Women's Pathways to Leadership and Empowerment
19. Feeling to Healing: The Role of Emotional Intelligence in Child Development
20. Transformative Talks and Words of Inspiration: Insights into Motivational Oratory

in a Complex World

Bhajan

101.  Pilgrimage of the Soul: Spiritual Journeys in India

❦❦❦

# Contact


Dr. Minakshi Bansal
Social Activist
Ahmedabad, Gujarat, Bharat
minakshiindiag20@yahoo.com


ᕛᕛᕛ

|| LOKAHA SAMASTHAHA SUKHINO BHAVANTU ||